A MULTI-SENSORY APPROACH
TO LANGUAGE ARTS FOR

# SPECIFIC LANGUAGE DISABILITY CHILDREN

A GUIDE FOR PRIMARY TEACHERS

BETH H. SLINGERLAND

Third Printing 1975

Educators Publishing Service, Inc.
75 MOULTON STREET, CAMBRIDGE, MASSACHUSETTS 02138

TO THE MEMORY

of

Anna Gillingham

and

Bessie Stillman

who redirected the course
of my entire life

and

TO THE MEMORY

of

Mary Persis Winne

whose early recognition of Specific
Language Disability problems in
children made possible my work with
Anna Gillingham and Bessie Stillman.

# FOREWORD

Specific Language Disability as a special and significant problem deserves increasing attention among teachers and administrators not only to parallel increasingly interested involvement of the medical profession in this organismic syndrome, but also because many student insufficiencies in communication unyielding to traditional remedial techniques undoubtedly will be recognized to stem from this relatively unfamiliar condition. No longer is it possible to condone ignorance by the professional teacher corps concerning this disability, its cause and indicated therapy. Too long has there been a "blind spot" in the teaching profession regarding the identification of this among the various patterns of individual differences. Educational techniques indicated for this unique group comprising approximately 10% of the identified reading and communication problems in American schools likewise are relatively unknown except in a few communities in the nation.

The author of this volume makes a comprehensive presentation of the precise techniques in education indicated by medically based insights concerning this genetically derived neurological under-development within the child. She is undoubtedly the most competent person available to make this presentation. These techniques are presented against a back-drop of concern for the total curriculum, especially the language and communicative arts as a unity and, therefore, do not single out a few "cure all" procedures as have some fads of the past which attempted to deal with this problem. This balanced and carefully scientific program has produced remarkable results in prototype schools where it has been tried with adequate professional help, including medical supervision. The rescue of many children with the symptoms of Specific Language Disability for school performance at a much higher level and approximating their estimated potential has been an expectancy and a fulfillment across the nation in selected schools where the program has been carefully tested.

Teacher education programs can no longer ignore this "blind spot." Knowledge and methodology concerning the syndrome of Specific Language Disability should become a necessary part of any sequence in which a student becomes acquainted with the wide variety of individual differences among children in schools and with the differentiated programs required to meet these differences in the context of the school program. The discovery of Specific Language Disability and how to mount successful therapeutic and educational programs for overcoming it likewise deserves the attention of in-service teachers and administrators. Both the training and retraining of teachers is indicated and should be initiated in classrooms on a grand scale without delay.

W. Ray Rucker, Dean
Graduate School of Leadership
    and Human Behavior
United States International University
San Diego, California

# FOREWORD

Proficiency in the skills of reading, writing, and spelling is necessary today as never before for one to be able to cope with the progression of his educational experience. A child who fails to acquire these basic skills is in serious trouble almost from the start of his schooling. Moreover, if this child fails despite adequate intellect, motivation, vision, and hearing, and becomes a poor reader, writer, or speller, his emotional well-being may be in jeopardy, as well as his education. The need for early identification of the child with Specific Language Disabilities cannot be overemphasized, for early recognition makes possible preventive measures as well as remedial education. The time-honored reminder of the relative values of prevention and cure has never been more appropriate than in the case of the child with SLD, for preventive measures may avert an emotional disaster for these children who may be keenly perceptive in all areas other than in language skills.

The need for the early identification of the child with SLD subserves the even greater need for starting the child as soon as possible in a very carefully designed program for language instruction in which special techniques and trained personnel are used to develop the simultaneous auditory, visual, and kinesthetic-motor integration which is indispensable for competence in language behavior. One such method devised by Mrs. Slingerland is an adaptation of the Orton-Gillingham approach for use in the classroom whereby one well-trained teacher is able to work with a class of children. The large number of children needing this kind of instruction calls for the most efficient use of trained teachers.

Although physicians, educators, and psychologists increasingly agree that this complex learning disorder is an interdisciplinary matter, it is also agreed that the problem can be solved mainly through the application of very special and structured teaching techniques. At the same time, it is recognized that cooperative medical and psychological resources should be available as needed for support of the teaching program. The desired goal is success for the child in the language skills. It is not sufficient that one should accept as a reasonable compromise that of a child who is a well adjusted poor reader.

The material presented in this book has been carefully designed and tested, and has been found to be useful in the hands of the trained classroom teacher. It is recommended to all who are concerned with the problem of teaching the language skills, at any level, as well as to those in the closely allied areas of medicine and psychology.

Wilbur E. Mattison, Jr., M.D.
President, The Board of Trustees
The Charles Armstrong School
1187 University Drive
Menlo Park, California 94025

# ACKNOWLEDGEMENTS

It would be impossible to acknowledge all who have provided the facilities, support, and experimental teaching that helped to bring about the development of this particular classroom instructional technique for the all too often unrecognized and misunderstood Specific Language Disability children.

Opportunity came to me in the mid-30's to discover why bright children could not seem to respond to methods of teaching reading, spelling, and writing found successful with other children of equal or even less intelligence. The early insight and recognition of disability by two educators—the late Mary Persis Winne, Principal of Punahou Elementary School, and Oscar F. Shepard, President, at that time, of Punahou School, Honolulu, Hawaii,—made possible my two years of study with Anna Gillingham and Bessie Stillman, and a relationship that brought lasting friendship and professional inspiration.

Oliver M. Hazen, Frank Monroe, and J.J. Pearce are among the first superintendents to recognize administration's obligation to provide the right "climate" under which SLD programs could go forward. Keith Allred and D. P. Langbell and others have followed.

Special commendation goes to those directly responsible for developing Specific Language Disability Programs,—the consultants, principals, and directors, such as Barbara Herman, Jean Raab, Belma Meeker, Nadyne Hill, Newton Manning, Nicholas Colasanti, Walter Key, Ennio Ciolli, Evelyn Buckley, all of whom attended teacher training summer sessions in addition to directing programs. Verna Rasmussen was responsible for the inception, with the follow-up support of the superintendent, Kedric W. Flint, of the Cut Bank, Montana SLD Program.

Encouragement and moral support has come at all times from the Presidents of the Orton Society, past and present—June L. Orton, Sally B. Childs, Margaret Rawson, and Roger Saunders.

Generous financial support was given by Charles E. Seay to assist Highland Park Independent School District, Dallas, Texas, in its initial teacher training program. In California, equally generous has been the Charles Dorsey Armstrong Memorial Foundation for similar support to Menlo Park City Schools and to The Armstrong School for SLD children. Because Specific Language Disability Programs depend upon trained teachers, their support was invaluable to this undertaking.

College credit for the four-week, all day summer courses, to introduce teachers and other school personnel to the background and techniques for Specific Language Disability has been given by Seattle Pacific College in Washington, East Texas State University in Texas, and by San Francisco State College and The College of Notre Dame, Belmont, in California. This enables many teachers to come from all over the United States and Canada.

For her many time consuming and helpful services to me while she was learning SLD techniques, special thanks go to Patricia M. Pease.

Most of all my gratitude is extended to the many classroom teachers whose basic understanding and skill with the techniques have prevented failure for many and restored self-confidence and successful learning for others who were failing. Without effort such as theirs, the best of research and study would never reach the children. My special commendation goes to Jean Raab, Barbara Herman, Martha Aho, Virginia Mason, Margaret

Pritchard, Eldra O'Neal, Helen Zylstra, Nicholas Colasanti, Patricia Cocoran Lopez, Cheery Howse, Elizabeth Hartley, Madge Lacey, Bessie Carter, Linda Scott, Joan Gott, Emily Scalese, Kathleen Titland, Thelma King and to many others.

Inspiration has come from working with and observing the wonderful SLD boys and girls themselves whose response is satisfying compensation for all the hours of effort and labor involved. Gratitude is extended to their parents, too, for all their encouragement, faith and active support.

Deserving of my most sincere appreciation is my husband, John, whose patient sacrifice of time and planned vacations have been delayed for the "cause" of Specific Language Disability children.

Beth H. Slingerland

# TABLE OF CONTENTS

DEDICATION                                                      iii

FOREWORD
    W. Ray Rucker                                          v
    Wilbur E. Mattison, Jr., M.D.                          vii

ACKNOWLEDGEMENTS                                                ix
TABLE OF CONTENTS                                               xi
MEMO FROM BETH H. SLINGERLAND                                   xiv
INTRODUCTION                                                    xv
PART 1—BACKGROUND
    Understanding Specific Language Disability             3
    The Need for Early Identification                      7
        TO THE TEACHER
    Division of the Language Arts Period                   9
    The Technique—Structured, not Programmed               10
    Phonics                                                11
    Why Manuscript Instead of Cursive is Used              13
    Not a Magic Method                                     14
    Group Therapy                                          15

PART 2—PREPARATIONS TO BE MADE BY THE TEACHER
    A Necessary Teacher Learning                           18
    Preparation of Materials
        Alphabet Wall Cards                                19
        Small Manuscript Alphabet Cards                    24
        Patterns for Tracing                               32
        Expendable Patterns                                33
        Classroom Equipment and Material                   34

PART 3—AUDITORY APPROACH AND LEARNING TO
WRITE FOR SPELLING AND WRITTEN EXPRESSION
    A Multi-Sensory Approach                               37
    Organization for Presenting Techniques                 39
    Learning to Write Letters of the Alphabet              40
    Structuring a New Learning—Consonants                  42
  A—ALPHABET CARDS
    Structuring a New Learning—Symbol-Sound Association    49
    Teaching More Consonants—Symbol-Sound                  52
    DAILY ORGANIZATION—Learning to Write, Auditory
        and Visual Approaches                              56
    Combining the Learning to Write and Auditory Approaches  58

Teaching *b* and *d* ............................................................ 62

Preventing Number Symbol Confusion ........................... 65

Structuring a New Learning—Vowels .............................. 66

Structuring a New Learning—Letter-size Relationship,
    Spacing and Alignment ............................................... 70

B—BLENDING

Structuring a New Learning—Blending to Form Word Entities ... 77

    EXAMPLE 1 of a Daily Lesson Plan ......................... 85

    EXAMPLE 2 of a Daily Lesson Plan ......................... 87

Introducing a New Vowel—Short *i* ............................... 90

Structuring a New Learning—Vowel Discrimination ......... 93

    EXAMPLE 3 of a Daily Lesson Plan ......................... 98

    EXAMPLE 4 of a Daily Lesson Plan ......................... 99

    EXAMPLE 5 of a Daily Lesson Plan ......................... 100

    EXAMPLE 6 of a Daily Lesson Plan ......................... 102

C—SPELLING

Planning Ahead .......................................................... 103

DAILY ORGANIZATION OF INSTRUCTION .................. 104

How to Use the Daily Organization for Planning ............. 106

Structuring a New Learning— Use of suffixes, with Concept—*ing* ... 108

    EXAMPLE 7 of a Daily Lesson Plan ......................... 113

Structuring Functional Use of Spelling—Phrases .............. 116

    EXAMPLE 8 of a Daily Lesson Plan ......................... 119

Structuring Functional Use of Spelling—Red Flag Words .... 121

    EXAMPLE 9 of a Daily Lesson Plan ......................... 124

Structuring Functional Use of Spelling—Sentences ........... 126

    EXAMPLE 10 of a Daily Lesson Plan ....................... 131

Structuring the Use of the Suffix *ed,* with "Past Time" Concept ... 133

Experiences to Reinforce Concept of Suffixes *ing* and
    *ed* and for Verbalizing Answers to Teacher Questions ... 136

Structuring the Use of Suffix *er* to Form Nouns .............. 138

Structuring the Use of *s* and *es* as Third Person Singular
    Suffixes, with Concept ............................................. 142

D—DICTATION ........................................................... 144

E—CREATIVE WRITTEN EXPRESSION AND INDE-
    PENDENT WORK .................................................... 144

SUMMARIZING PROGRESS AND LOOKING AHEAD ... 145


PART 4—THE VISUAL APPROACH FOR READING

Procedures ................................................................. 151

DAILY ORGANIZATION OF INSTRUCTION .................. 153

    Learning to Write .................................................... 154

A—ALPHABET CARDS ................................................. 154

Structuring the Use of Alphabet Cards ........................... 154

B—UNLOCKING WORDS ....................................................... 157
    Structuring the First Use of Consonants for Unlocking Words ........ 157
    Structuring a New Learning— Unlocking One-Syllable,
        Short Vowel *a* Phonetic Words ................................... 160
    Unlocking Words That END With More Than One Consonant ........ 164
    Unlocking One-Syllable, Phonetic Words With Short *i* ............. 165
    A New Learning—Discrimination of Short Vowel *a* and *i* ........ 166
    Unlocking Words that BEGIN With More Than One Consonant ...... 168
    A New Learning—Unlocking One-Syllable Words Con-
        taining Vowel Digraphs, Diphthongs and Phonograms ......... 170
    Reading ......................................................... 174
C—PREPARATION FOR READING—Words and Phrases ............. 175
    For Word Recognition—the four steps ........................... 176
    For Phrase Recognition—the four steps .......................... 180
D—READING FROM A BOOK ............................................ 185
    Procedures for Structuring the Reading ......................... 185
    Procedures for Advancing Progress ............................. 189
        Asking and Answering Questions—Verbalizing ............... 189
        Preventing *b* and *d* Confusion ............................ 191
        Studying aloud ........................................... 192
        Independent Study ........................................ 193
        Prepositions and Articles .................................. 194
        Unlocking Words .......................................... 197
    EXAMPLES OF DAILY LESSONS ................................. 
        Pre-primer level .......................................... 199
        Primer level .............................................. 212
        First grade level .......................................... 221
        First grade level (two groups) ............................. 224
    SUMMARIZING PROGRESS AND LOOKING AHEAD ............ 231
    BIBLIOGRAPHY ................................................. 235

Memo from: *Beth H. Slingerland*

This book describes the sequence of structured techniques and procedures for teaching Specific Language Disability Children. However, no written explanation of a teaching method is ever an adequate substitute for training. You will be able to learn the techniques, but you are in *no* way adequately prepared to teach a class of SLD children in this method without first completing one of the Slingerland teacher training programs. Slingerland training programs are therefore offered in a number of cities throughout the country to meet the needs of teachers working with SLD pupils.

The only approved training centers are located in the areas listed below. The programs are devoted in their entirety to introducing the multi-sensory teaching techniques of the Slingerland classroom adaptation of the Orton-Gillingham approach. Those who attend will gain background and training and an understanding of the basic principles which underlie the instructional method.

While attending, the participants:

1. Observe experienced staff teachers give daily demonstrations with children in classroom situations.
2. Work with individual children to learn and gain confidence in the use of the instructional techniques under guidance from the staff.
3. Gain knowledge of the neurological background, the instructional techniques and sequential phonics in the daily lecture periods.
4. Make their own materials for use in classrooms (or with individual children) and in so doing, the techniques are reinforced.

All of the Slingerland training programs are four weeks in length with daily schedules from approximately 8:00 a.m. to 3:00 p.m. Participants receive graduate credit upon completion of the four-week program.

Slingerland teacher-training programs are regularly conducted in the following locations.

| | | | |
|---|---|---|---|
| ALASKA: | CONNECTICUT: | OHIO: | WASHINGTON: |
| Anchorage | West Hartford | Cleveland | Mount Vernon |
| CALIFORNIA: | MARYLAND: | OREGON: | Renton |
| Cupertino | Baltimore | Medford | Richland |
| Menlo Park | MASSACHUSETTS: | Portland | Shoreline |
| San Diego | Cape Cod | TEXAS: | Whidby Island |
| San Mateo | MONTANA: | Dallas | Yakima |
| Santa Rosa | Kalispell | Everman | |
| | | Richardson | |

Reports on the achievement of children taught by this method and addresses of Slingerland approved training centers are available from:

THE SLINGERLAND INSTITUTE

c/o Manter Hall School          or          23600 Marine View Drive
71 Mount Auburn Street                               Seattle, Washington 98188
Cambridge, Massachusetts 02138

# INTRODUCTION

The teaching technique to be presented herein is for use as a preventive or early remedial measure with Specific Language Disability (SLD)* or Specific Developmental Dyslexic children in the primary grades. Realizing the impossibility of giving individual instruction to most of the children in public school classroom situations, the technique was developed as a group therapy. It is an adaptation for classroom use of the ORTON-GILLINGHAM** approach to reading, writing and spelling. Because language depends on an intersensory functioning, meaning a neurological organization for automatic linkage of auditory-visual-kinesthetic impressions within the human brain, the underlying basic principles upon which this technique is organized are multi-sensory. The object is to foster simultaneous or automatic auditory-visual-kinesthetic (A-V-K) association, regardless of which modality † carries the initial stimulus. For example, with a letter of the alphabet, a basic instructional technique used to strengthen association of the three sensory pathways, and for their integration and recall, is for the teacher to expose the letter for *visual perception*, and for a child, while keeping his eyes on the letter, immediately to form the letter with an arm swing from the shoulder (kinesthetic-motor), at the same time he gives its *name and sound* (auditory)—a kinesthetic-auditory association with the initial visual stimulus. (Refer to pages 52 through 55.) Another example, to "fix" reading vocabulary, *after the words (or phrases have been presented by the teacher,* is for her to name one of a group of exposed words (or phrases) for *auditory perception* and for the child, associating the heard word with its visual

---

*Dyslexia means defective reading. There is much disagreement regarding the term dyslexia as applied to children having language problems. Some believe there is no constitutional basis for this disorder. Others believe there is a genetic origin that accounts for what many of us in education prefer to speak of as Specific Language Disability. A definition given by the WORLD FEDERATION OF NEUROLOGY, Research Group on Developmental Dyslexia and World Illiteracy, meeting in Dallas, Texas, April 3, 4, 5, 1968, is as follows:

> SPECIFIC DEVELOPMENTAL DYSLEXIA: A disorder manifested by difficulty in learning to read despite conventional instruction, adequate intelligence, and socio-cultural opportunity. It is dependent upon fundamental cognitive disabilities which are frequently of constitutional origin.

This definition underlies the basic principles upon which the Orton-Gillingham approach was presented.

**The Orton-Gillingham approach, using a systematic presentation of oral and written language, begins with single symbols or "units" of sight-sound-feel—letters of the alphabet—and builds these into one-syllable words or "units", and then, proceeding on to more-than-one-syllable words, eventually leads to their automatic recognition when organized into phrases, sentences and paragraphs—units of concept. Each step emphasizes the reinforcement of learning through the integrated impressions carried over the three sensory channels of audition, vision and kinesthesis. Frequently the approach is misunderstood, misinterpreted, even misrepresented, by those with insufficient background and training for an understanding of the basic principles which underlie the instructional technique. It is an approach that offers great flexibility in meeting individual need and in bringing forth the imagination and creativity found in many SLD children.

† Modalities are visual, auditory, and kinesthetic sensory pathways so organized to carry the symbolic stimuli of language to or from the brain. A child with competence in each of the modalities is not likely to have any difficulty with learning to read, write and spell. In others, a weakness in one modality may or may not be compensated by the strength of another. If not, then for some, a dysfunctioning of intersensory

counterpart, to point to the word (visual-auditory association) and to read it aloud (kinesthetic association)—an auditory-visual-kinesthetic linkage. (Refer to pages 176 through 178.) Individual weaknesses in any one of the channels of perception or in the integration process for concept and retention may require emphasis to be placed on the association of the weak with the strong modality. The instructional therapy to be found in Teaching Procedures, Part 3 and Part 4 is built around the linkage or association of all three pathways to aid in the necessary final integrative process required for intelligent reading, for spelling, for penmanship, and for written expression.

There is no intention of presenting this technique as the *only way* to assist Specific Language Disability children with their various and varying degrees of disability. It is *one way* and a way that can be used with classes of children as well as with small groups, or even an individual. It should not, however, be combined with other techniques or methods or the best results will be lost. In fairness to whatever approach is used, and to the *children*, adherence to the chosen one is recommended. But, there is little time within a busy day's schedule for a teacher to use several different techniques without leaving too many children of primary ages "on their own" to form bad habits of wasting time. Therefore, grouping SLD children to be taught by one appropriate instructional method is a means of bringing about successful learning which eventually provides children with the tools for working "on their own."

There is firm backing for early identification with a follow-up in instructional therapy designed for Specific Language Disability needs. In one publication Leon Eisenberg, M.D.,[26]* Professor of Child Psychiatry, writes:

> . . . It is essential that we early identify the child who will not succeed to read on time (DeHirsch, Jansky, Langford, 1965). The child not beginning to read by the second semester of the first grade needs diagnostic study and appropriate remedial education. If to achieve this means that we will be giving extra help to a child who does not need it, then I urge that we do so. The surplus child will not be harmed and may be benefitted; the dyslexic child will be reached at a time the chance of success is greatest. . . .

Dr. Gilbert Schiffman,[72] former State Supervisor of Reading in Maryland, found in a major survey, that with special help for a given period of time 82% of children identified in

---

integration prevents compensation and specific language disability is apt to be the result. Still other children have weakness in more than one modality and they usually show extreme disability.

The technique of instruction will determine to a large extent both success or failure. Emphasis needs to be placed on the association of the weak modality with the stronger. Phonics benefits those with weak visual modalities. Much repetition of what is *heard* and *felt*, with "over-teaching", helps those with weakness in auditory and auditory-kinesthetic modalities. When both auditory and visual modalities are weak, a combination of emphases is mandatory. The adaptation of the Orton-Gillingham approach as it is presented in this book is based on these needs. Ideally, and to be hoped for some future time, modality weakness and strength will determine the placement of all SLD children into groups where those with similar modality weakness or weaknesses can be given the kinds of instructional emphasis most effective for them.

*NOTE: Numbers refer to entry in Bibliography—pages 235-239.

first and second grades maintain grade level if the help begins immediately. The percentage drops to 46% when treatment begins in the third grade. Recovery drops sharply when treatment is delayed until fifth and sixth grades when percentages fall to 18% and 8%, respectively.

It is possible to identify pre-schoolers without waiting for them to begin to fail to learn to read. This can be done by administering individual tests[21] or by screening groups[80] of from 10-15 children at one time when individual diagnosis is not possible.

Identification calls for appropriate "preventive" instructional therapy. To present one such therapy is the purpose of this book.

A MULTI-SENSORY APPROACH
TO LANGUAGE ARTS FOR

# SPECIFIC
# LANGUAGE
# DISABILITY
# CHILDREN

A GUIDE FOR PRIMARY TEACHERS

# PART 1

## BACKGROUND

## UNDERSTANDING SPECIFIC LANGUAGE DISABILITY

Prerequisite to successful use of the teaching technique contained in Part 3 of this book is some understanding of Specific Language Disability.

Recommended reading is to be found in the BIBLIOGRAPHY FOR TEACHERS OF CHILDREN WITH DYSLEXIA OR SPECIFIC LANGUAGE DISABILITY, pages 235-239.

Specific Language Disability—dyslexia, developmental dyslexia, word blindness, strephosymbolia—or whatever label is preferred for the intelligent children with communicative disorders has been explained in the following way by Dr. Raymond Clemmons, Department of Pediatrics, University of Maryland School of Medicine:[16]*

> *An exact definition* of specific language disability is not possible since the disorder ranges in degree from the very mild to the extremely severe. The key point, however, is that reading and language skills are definitely out of keeping with overall intellectual capacities and that this difference persists in spite of competent instruction over adequate periods of time with pedagogical methods which are successful in the majority of children. It is in this regard, namely the failure to learn at the usual rates by the usual pedagogic methods, that the term "specific" is appropriate.

Without necessarily knowing causes or having the background for understanding the problem, teachers long have been aware of the Specific Language Disability syndrome. Its familiar symptoms are characteristic of some 10-20% of children whose achievement in reading, writing, spelling and both oral and written language is not commensurate with intelligence or abilities in other areas such as science and mathematics. Even without diagnosis teachers can recognize some of the symptoms that occur in the SLD syndrome, all of which, however, are not necessarily found in any one child. A child:

1. may be a very poor reader, failing completely.

2. may read below intellectual capacity and ability to comprehend what is spoken or read aloud by someone else.

3. may lose the thought in the struggle with the mechanics of reading, insert or omit words, guess, ignore phrasing, punctuation marks.

4. may learn to read, or to read well enough to "get by" in elementary school only to collapse when junior high is reached.

5. may read at "grade level" but not commensurate with intelligence.

6. may avoid reading if possible and not read for pleasure.

7. may read, but fail in spelling.

*NOTE: numbers refer to entry in Bibliography—pages 235-239.

8. may not read or spell.

9. may learn to spell a "list" of words sufficiently well to "pass" on weekly tests, but forget them all by Monday to make way for the new list.

10. may be unable to spell previously "memorized" words in dictated sentences or in propositional written expressions.

11. may leave out or insert letters, misplace, add or omit whole syllables.

12. may have poor use of syntax, prefixes, suffixes.

13. may have adequate ability to express self orally, but almost none for written expression.

14. may mispronounce, misuse or fail to retain words for verbal use.

15. may lose concept by misreading or misunderstanding similarly appearing or sounding words—country-county; historical-hysterical.

16. may have difficulty understanding what is read aloud or in comprehending directions.

17. may have difficulty answering questions or in describing something which carries over into unsatisfactory written work.

18. may struggle to recall sequential movement patterns necessary for automatic letter formation, resulting in poor and disordered written work.

19. may know *how to form* the letters, but not to recall *which letters to use* in spelling so penmanship and neatness suffer.

20. may be unable to remember words and phrases as they are dictated.

This list, while incomplete, will undoubtedly call forth mental pictures of many children whose struggles have frustrated the best efforts of excellent teachers using conventional methods successful with the majority. To these language difficulties may be added poor behavioral and attitudinal and emotional problems, feelings of inadequacy, loss of self respect and tragic, indeed, loss of status among peers. Sometimes parental disappointment, blame or condemnation compounds the problem. Unfortunately, when there is unfamiliarity with or misconception of Specific Language Disability by school personnel, language problems may be considered secondary to the emotional overlay. Writes Elena Boder, M.D., Associate Clinical Professor of Pediatrics, School of Medicine, U.C.L.A. in Los Angeles:[8]

.... The older child referred to the clinic as a "non-reader" had invariably proved to have specific dyslexia. The application of this term to the child by school personnel has therefore come to be viewed by the writer as virtually diagnostic.

. . . . . . . . . . . .

.... Specific dyslexia, like the anxiety it produces, appears in many disguises and mimics many behavioral disorders; for example, dyslexic children are more frequently referred to the neurology clinic for behavior problems rather than for a reading problem. Their reading disorder tends to be viewed as secondary to their behavioral problems and they are, therefore, often misjudged as being poorly motivated, not interested in reading or uncooperative.

Too often the reasons for inadequate performance have been sought in purely psychological or extraneous influences affecting the child such as home, social or economic environment, poor teaching, irregular school attendance. Certainly negative influences, where they exist, cannot be disregarded, but it is of equal importance to note the number of children who *do* learn in spite of their subjection to the same kinds of negative influences.[31] Fortunate it is for SLD boys and girls of the present and future that leaders within the various disciplines of medical, psychiatric and educational fields are bringing their forces together to interrelate the findings of each. The need for this is pointed out in what Dr. Ralph Rabinovitch, Director of Hawthorn Center, Northville, Michigan, has to say:[62]

...So often the school social worker or pediatrician refers the child with the hope, and even expectations, that the psychiatric clinic will find the learning problem to be due to an "emotional block" and that through the magic of psychotherapy, perhaps limited to a few interviews, the child will be "released" to learn adequately. Such unrealistic expectations have, unfortunatley, been fostered in part by the attitude of some of our own colleagues in child psychiatry and related fields who have been prone to overgeneralize dynamic formulations. The problem is far more complex; and the understanding of the large mass of reading problems which we see represents, I believe, one of the major current challenges to our field.

To many, Specific Language Disability is believed to be of biologic or endogenous origin, predetermined by familial (some say hereditary) neurological disorganization in the central nervous system's handling of language symbols, and not to be blamed on anyone— not the parent, not the child, not the teacher and not the school system. It is just the way some are born.

Development of cognition as expressed through language depends upon a "three-fold" language pattern [32,57] —the automatic association or linking of stimuli as they are carried over visual-auditory-kinesthetic sensory channels to the cortex of the brain, under control of the central nervous system. There, the incoming impressions carried over these modalities of "input" go through a complex process of integration for storage in association with concept and past stimuli, being held somehow for delayed recall and then formed into motor patterns so they can be sent over sensory channels of "output." This is an important learning for SLD teachers because *presenting* new steps is not enough. Children need help *with the integrative process* by fostering associations, strengthening A-V-K linkages, and *how* to recall, with practice in so doing. Practice is not just "assignment," but often requires the teacher to stand by to give help where the need is indicated. *To prevent mistakes, not to correct mistakes,* is an essential approach for good SLD teaching.

Teachers learn that somehow, in SLD children, without brain damage, certain maturational language patternings have failed to reach full functional physiological development, spoken of as "neurophysiological dysfunctioning." For the large majority, this "patterning" for language perception, integration and recall follows well ordered paths that serve man's language needs throughout life. Dr. Wilder Penfield,[60] neurologist, tells us they are usually established by approximately twelve years of age.

When developmental lags occur some children fail to reach certain anticipated points in the over-all patterns of maturation. Dr. Lauretta Bender[7] points out that:

> . . . Areas of the brain cortex serving such specifically human functions related to unilateral dominance as hand preference in using tools and in writing, and in learning processes for speaking, reading, spelling and written language show a wider range in time of maturation than do other maturational habit patterns. . . . . .

There may be delay, but where there is no known brain damage or impairment, there can be response to structured patterning. Developmental lag which persists on beyond acceptable periods of delay may be due to specific language disability which may not correct itself without help in coping with the disability. With this in mind, teachers should not overlook or minimize the need for structuring and patterning each progressive learning step.

Dyslexic or SLD children's problems are at last being brought into focus, their needs recognized. When the etiology is fully understood, education will continue to have the final responsibility for the success or failure of these children. This is expressed by Dr. Wilbur Mattison, Jr.* "We have no difficulty finding the dyslexic child. How to provide adequate training or retraining is our problem." Medical and psychiatric research can bring about better understanding and knowledge of the dyslexic or SLD children, but education must provide the therapy.

*Dr. Wilbur Mattison, Jr., Director, Charles Dorsey Armstrong Memorial Foundation, Menlo Park, California.

## THE NEED FOR EARLY IDENTIFICATION

The advisability of early identification of children with SLD is gaining the recognition it deserves. Early catchment and prevention is advocated by many authorities, one of whom, Dr. Rabinovitch,[62] writes:

> . . . Our experience at Hawthorn indicates dramatically the need for early intervention, as close to first grade level as possible.

Another is Dr. Leon Eisenberg: [26]

> . . . An effective program for early identification and treatment might even produce long-run savings if we take into account the cost of prolonged treatment and the ultimate loss in economic productivity of handicapped readers.

Dr. Gilbert Schiffman states:[71]

> . . . Of course the best remediation is not a revised curriculum or more reading personnel, but early identification.

> . . . . . . . .

> Emphasis must be placed upon early identification and placement in the proper program before an individual's problem becomes too complex.

> If the child cannot be identified and remediated on the elementary level, what chance does he have in the complex secondary program? No longer can teachers afford to wait for the child to be referred for special help only after continued academic failure, "atypical" behavior or efforts of "over-aggressive" parents. Early identification and preventive practices are the only solution.

Recognition of the SLD syndrome after children fail has led to the advisability of identifying language disabilities before the introduction of reading, writing, and spelling begins. The importance of knowing what point each pre-school child has reached in the anticipated maturational steps of language development when entering school cannot be minimized or assumed to be adequate.

Language follows a continuum in development from birth onward. A child is born without any language and, assuming there is no brain damage, with a brain ready to develop the sensory pathways or modalities that enable stimuli to be carried to the cortex of the brain for the complex neurological processing that leads to understanding, speaking, reading, and written language. The infant hears sounds that become familiar and are recognized as they are carried over the auditory sensory channel. Soon, symbolic sounds of speech are associated with initial concepts. Then comes the "feel" of speech in learning to talk. During the first six to seven years, the *hearing* and *speaking*, in association with what is seen and understood in the environment, is of prime importance as pre-requisites for reading.

Some beginners enter school sadly deficient in their understood and speaking vocabularies. They do not know or do not recall the names (anomia) of objects seen in everyday life.

Some are unable to express themselves or to speak in more than monosyllables, frequently pointing or grunting in hopes they will be understood. Many show auditory-motor dysfunctioning: unable to put their bodies into the necessary motor performance following verbal directions; i.e., to "put the spoon on the plate," or, as with first graders, to "put your finger on the top line, and then *point* to each line as you count one, two, three, down to the third line." Consequently, they need experience to enrich the understanding and use of the symbolic language of *sound* and its *feel* and for motor performance to follow an auditory stimulus. Opportunity for such developmental steps should come before superimposing the written symbols of sight needed for reading.[91]*

Other beginners, strong in the verbal and auditory-motor avenues have difficulties with perception and recall of written symbols. They lose the correct sequencing of letters within words so that the perception and retention of "word wholes" is confused and unreliable. They may lack good eye-hand coordination and fail to remember the sequential movement patterns in forming letters, all of which interferes with learning to read and to write.

All these children are in need of early identification and appropriate preventive training to insure as much success as possible in their first attempts to achieve and to gain positive psychological reaction to learning.

*Beth H. Slingerland, *Training in Some Prerequisites for Beginning Reading,* Cambridge, Mass., Educators Publishing Service, Inc., 1967.

TO THE TEACHER

**DIVISION OF THE LANGUAGE ARTS PERIODS—Two Separate Blocks of Time: The Auditory Approach—including the Auditory—Kinesthetic Approach and The Visual Approach**

The daily period allowed for the teaching of reading, hand-writing, spelling and written work is divided into two entirely separate lessons—THE VISUAL APPROACH and the AUDITORY APPROACH. The AUDITORY APPROACH includes the AUDITORY-KINESTHETIC APPROACH. Each approach leads to the simultaneous association of auditory-visual-kinesthetic impressions, a functioning for which SLD children often need special help.

In any VISUAL APPROACH - READING—, the initial stimuli come through the eyes to be carried over the visual sensory channel to the cortex of the brain. Words are perceived in simultaneous association with their sounds and with meaning. (While *copying* begins with the visual stimuli, requiring eye-hand coordination, it does not necessarily lead to reading or to understanding of what the words mean.)

In the AUDITORY APPROACH, including the AUDITORY-KINESTHETIC (A-K)—oral and written spelling—, the initial stimuli come through the ear to be carried over the auditory sensory channel to the brain. What is heard (hopefully) is simultaneously associated with concept, and with the *visual* graphic patterns for reading or spelling and the *kinesthetic-motor* patterns for speech and for writing. Usually what is to be written is *heard* when dictated by the teacher or from *self-direction* proposed by the child. This requires an auditory-visual-kinesthetic linkage. *In written work no word is actually seen with the eyes until produced.*

It is true that when a list of spelling words is presented *for study* the words are seen first. However, for functional use words to be written are heard inwardly, automatically transposed to their graphic appearances *and then written*. Not until this final step are words actually seen for reading. Specific Language Disability children, whose automatic association of sight, sound and "feel" is somehow dysfunctioning, often must be taught to make *conscious* effort to perceive, match and recall auditory-visual-kinesthetic impressions in association with each other.

## THE TECHNIQUE—STRUCTURED, NOT PROGRAMMED

None of the structured steps are presented in day-to-day programmed procedures. Each new learning is introduced through structured steps which lead the children to independent performance *after they can follow a "thought pattern"* as a guide.

1. When something is to be learned, it is introduced by the teacher with *demonstration and discussion* to foster understanding.

2. Individual children perform while the class watches, and when necessary, the teacher *guides the child's thought* through each step *before* performance *to prevent* failure and to lead the child to final success. (This requires an auditory-motor performance.)

3. In another lesson, all children may work independently. The teacher directs their thinking through each step wherever children appear to need further direction to *prevent* errors before they are made. The object is *to prevent*, not *to correct*. To accomplish this the teacher must circulate among the children while they are working to give immediate guidance, reassurance and confirmation. *Teaching* and being available during first experiences in handling new steps and concepts is the SLD classroom teacher's vital role.

4. Providing opportunity to work without help or to test is the final step in structuring. The goal is reached when children have learned to carry a given learning to successful completion with self-dependence and self-confidence.

   If a few of the children cannot succeed, then a few more teacher-directed lessons may be in order. If many are unsure, the teacher may conclude that not enough guidance and directed experience in actual performance was provided before expecting the children to work "on their own."

5. The ultimate goal, understandably, is to be able to use what has been learned when its need in any situation arises.

# PHONICS *

Phonics is a necessary part of the training procedures for Specific Language Disability children, but not a goal unto itself. Teachers must learn to use phonetic sounds, or phonemes,** in isolation correctly before attempting to teach by following adaptation for classroom use. Otherwise the teacher will fail in the use of the technique which has been used successfully for over thirty years.

Unlike the majority of children who can learn words as "wholes," SLD boys and girls cannot depend upon their perceptions, retention and recall of words as "constant" entities of sight and/or sound. To them the letters or syllables of a word may become disorganized in their spatial and/or temporal relationships. Some perceive well enough to get concept so "they read" after a fashion, but they may fail to recognize the words out of context or in other reading material, and have no means of "unlocking" them. Spelling, which requires exact recall of letter positioning, is even more difficult.

The "preventive" or early remedial therapy begins with a *single unit* of sight, sound and "feel," soon to be synthesized into "whole word units." From letters as "single units," the teaching procedure leads to phonetic one-syllable, short vowel words or syllables as "larger single units." Following this learning *with practice,* these word or syllable "units" are combined to form more than one syllable words that come to be recognized as even larger "units" or "wholes." In time, even these polysyllabic words can be recalled instantly or can be worked out for reading and for spelling if unrecognized.

Combining an "intellectual" and phonetic approach is stressed. As an example, if dependent on phonics alone, the child might spell *jumped*—j-u-m-p-t—which is the way it *sounds.* When spelling "through the intellect" the child learns to think of the root word with its meaning and how it is spelled. By saying "jumped," the need to add the suffix that makes the root word mean what happened "before now" or in the past, calls for the suffix *ed* regardless of its sound which can be /d/ as in snowed; /ĕd/ as in planted; or /t/ as in jumped. Early training such as this begins in first grade. It provides the basis for later "intellectual" learning of generalizations and rules by the time intermediate grades are reached.

Auditory and visual perception and recall of *vowel sounds* within words and syllables serves as *the key for "unlocking."* It becomes a *basic learning.*

How to strengthen recognition and recall of non-phonetic words is another *basic training.*

---

*Beth H. Slingerland, *Phonetic Word Lists for Children's Use,* and *Teacher's Word Lists for Reference,* Cambridge, Mass., Educators Publishing Service, Inc., 1969.

** *Phonemes* are basic sound units from which words are made.
  In our language some phonemes may be spelled in different ways, e.g., /ĕ/ may be spelled *e* as in *red* or *ea* as in *head.*
*Graphemes* are their visual or written counterparts.

Phonemes, or sound units, are introduced through the Auditory Approach first, with visual-kinesthetic association. Unless there is impairment of auditory acuity, the initial steps begin as an auditory perception. Not until the synthesis, or blending, of *single units of sound* (spelling) into "whole words" is comprehended and functional, should there be any introduction of "whole words" to be *changed into sound* (reading) by finding *what makes the vowel sound* and then resynthesizing. FIRST GRADERS' <u>INTRODUCTION TO READING</u> PER SE NEED NOT WAIT UNTIL WORDS CAN BE "UNLOCKED" FOR INDEPENDENT ATTACK, BUT CAN BEGIN AT THE SAME TIME THEY ARE LEARNING HOW TO SPELL WORDS FROM THE LETTERS THAT HAVE BEEN TAUGHT. (Refer to page 151.)

By the second year children can use diphthongs, digraphs, phonograms* and letter combinations *in reading much more rapidly than in spelling*. The "units" or wholes that make the vowel sounds, such as *ee, oa, igh,* etc., are recognized, the word unlocked with concept (it is hoped) and reading continues as an "input" function. The instant there is recognition and comprehension there is no need for exact recall of letter sequence. This is not true in spelling because exact letter sequencing must be recalled as part of "output" function. To further complicate spelling, vowel sounds can be spelled in several ways. Learning to use phonics can be expected to provide quicker results with reading than with spelling. More time and use of the multi-sensory approach may be required with severe spelling disabilities.

---

\* A *diphthong* is a speech sound that changes continuously from one vowel sound to another in the same syllable, e.g., *oi, ai, ou.*

A *digraph* may be formed by two vowels or two consonants representing a single speech sound, e.g., *sh-/sh/; kn-/n/; ph-/f/; ee-/ē/; oo-/o͞o/ and /o͝o/.*

A *phonogram* is a symbol or combination of symbols that represent a single speech sound, such as g, f, ph, igh, ar, ai, oy, etc.

A *letter combination* is a group of letters that is learned as an auditory or sound "whole" and as a visual or graphic "unit," e.g., ing, unk, ang, tion, sion.

## WHY MANUSCRIPT INSTEAD OF CURSIVE IS USED

The Orton-Gillingham approach recommends that teaching cursive rather than manuscript begin in the first year, thereby avoiding any need to change from manuscript to cursive at a later time, and because cursive letter forms flow more rhythmically from letter to letter and are less apt to be reversed. Therefore, if a school or school system begins with cursive, the same techniques given herein are applicable. HOW WRITING SYMBOLS ARE TAUGHT RATHER THAN WHICH FORMS ARE USED, IS THE PRIMARY FACTOR IN THIS APPROACH. Most public schools throughout the country, however, use manuscript for the first two or three years, at least.

When making this adaptation for classroom use in public school situations from the Orton-Gillingham approach, it was considered better to conform to accepted practices whenever and wherever possible. To minimize any chance of confusion or interference with school district policies, manuscript, instead of cursive, was used.

Some other factors *in favor* of manuscript brought about this decision.

1. The type for letter forms used in the basic readers is more like manuscript than cursive in appearance. (Differences such as a — a, and g — g, are pointed out to the children and explained if confusion is suspected.)

2. Manuscript should be used by the teacher in preparing materials and when writing on the blackboard, enabling SLD groups of children to see the same symbol forms used for reading, spelling, and handwriting, thereby lessening confusion and the need for too many new learnings close together.

3. If primary children who are being taught by this multi-sensory technique must be transferred to other schools or communities wherein they will not have this same training, they still will not be confronted with a change in letter forms. If, however, they have had cursive instead of manuscript, they might be expected to make the change-over *without special retraining,* something that could compound the difficulties and confusions that probably placed them in an SLD Program in the first place.

Note: Manuscript letter forms are taught so each letter is formed with one single stroke wherever possible and not with the usual circle and line such as Non-SLD children can learn. This is to minimize directional confusion. (Refer to page 40 — and on.)

*When the Change-Over from Manuscript to Cursive is Introduced*

The change-over from manuscript to cursive is presented at the beginning of the third year. Experience has shown that the children are highly motivated for this new learning and that the third year offers excellent opportunity for review of spelling techniques at the same time the cursive letter forms are being learned for functional use. Cursive writing receives the same structured guidance as was given to manuscript in the first years. It serves as a basic step in the third year continuum of this plan of instruction, similar in function to that of manuscript for beginners. When introduced at this time it is especially beneficial for children entering an SLD program for the first time.*

*The third and fourth years in the continuum of this instructional technique for SLD children will be explained under separate cover at a future date.

## NOT A MAGIC METHOD

If instant or "showy" results are anticipated from using this technique, the teacher or parent with such expectations should look elsewhere. Only acquired skill in its use, patience and persistence on the part of the teacher, and with faith in the child's desire to learn regardless of how indifferent or resistant he may seem at first, brings about the desired ends. The writer, after thirty years of experience, knows of no magic touch to offer as a means to quick results. Many children have shown remarkable changes in attitude and self-esteem along with learning ability, within an amazingly short time, but others may take longer. It is to be expected that about two years of help are necessary before children can work independently to maintain grade level. It may take longer, depending upon *when the therapy begins*, and upon *previous failures* that have added overlays of emotional blockages and attitudinal and behavioral problems. Of course, *intelligence,* the *degree of disability,* and *inner drive* are vital factors.

If much that appears herein seems repetitious, it is because teachers who have attended SLD summer schools and work in SLD classrooms during the year have repeatedly asked for "repetition" to strengthen their own understanding and automatic use of the technique's sequential and systematic steps for structuring children's thought and performance patterns.

## SPECIFIC LANGUAGE DISABILITY CLASSES AFFORD GROUP THERAPY

Experience has shown that children working together, all of whom have borderline to severe degrees of SLD, have provided a desirable therapy of their own. Being with others whose learning difficulties are the same and knowing there is understanding and tolerance for their inadequacies does much to foster or to restore self confidence, build positive attitudes and to lessen fears of failure.

By grouping SLD first grade beginners together they do not experience failure as they do when placed with equally bright non-SLD children whose ability to out distance them is disconcerting and frustrating.

SLD children respond to sympathetic encouragement while being shown how to achieve. They do not necessarily respond to praise until they know, inwardly, that they are succeeding and that their achievement, no matter how small, justifies teacher praise as sincere.

Spontaneous recognition of successful performance by classmates has provided highly effective psychological therapy.

# PART 2

PREPARATIONS

TO BE MADE
BY THE TEACHER

# TEACHER PREPARATION

## A NECESSARY TEACHER LEARNING—
## Recognizing and Reproducing Correct Sounds of Phonemes

Any teacher of Specific Language Disability children must know how to make the correct sounds of each consonant, vowel, consonant and vowel digraph, diphthong, phonogram and letter combination.

Any person who does not hear well or cannot use sounds correctly, possibly due to speech impediment, should not try to become an SLD teacher. (Refer to pages 21-23 and 28-30.)
Foreign accents are a hindrance when teaching SLD English speaking children.

Cassettes that give the consonant and vowel pronunciations can be purchased.* To know the correct sounds is *a necessary learning* on the part of teachers.

As an example, *b* does not have the sound /buh/ which, when pronounced in this way is followed by the short *u* sound. The sound of a *b* can be *heard* and *felt* when the words *rub* and *big* are pronounced. *Rub* is not pronounced ru-*buh*, nor is *big* pronounced *buh*-ig. None of the pure consonant sounds should include any vowel sound. (Refer to pages 22-23.)

*Sally B., and Ralph de S. Childs, *Sounds of English,* Cambridge, Mass., Educators Publishing Service, Inc., 1962.

# PREPARATION OF MATERIALS

### Alphabet Wall Cards

These cards are approximately 8 x 10 or 9 x 12 inches.

The Alphabet Wall Cards are usually prepared by the teacher. They are for wall placement to serve as an easy reference for children.

Examples of key-picture and lettering arrangement on the Wall Cards are given below and on the next page. (Refer to page 40.)

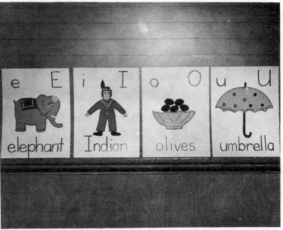

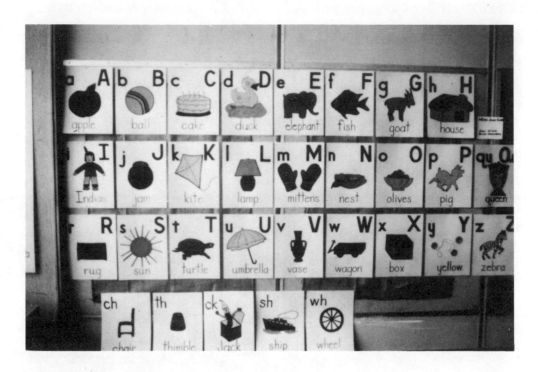

By Joan Gott

By Patricia Pease

For Wall Cards, highly recommended and most effective are key word picture patterns cut from felt cloth, then trimmed with sequins, if desired, and pasted on the cards. They are durable, colorful and they reflect no light.*

If preferred, colored pictures can be obtained from magazines, but this usually takes longer. Pictures can also be cut from ABC books.

Commercially prepared cards for wall display with key word pictures are available.**

Below is given the letter of the alphabet and a key word with the sound to be taught.

| Letter | Key Word | Something about the sound to be taught |
|--------|----------|----------------------------------------|
| *VOWELS* | | |
| a | *apple* | /ă/ |
| e | *elephant* | /ĕ/ |
| i | *Indian* | /ĭ/ |
| o | *olives* | /ŏ/ (*not* ostrich, which is often mispronounced) |
| u | *umbrella* | /ŭ/ |

*The ideas for using felt material and for most of the patterns must be credited to Eldra O'Neal and Helen Zylstra.
**Beth H. Slingerland, *Alphabet Wall Cards,* Cambridge, Mass., Educators Publishing Service, Inc., 1974.

21

| Letter | Key Word | Something about the sound to be taught |
|--------|----------|----------------------------------------|
| CONSONANTS | | |
| b | ball or baby | /b/, not / buh/ |
| c | cake | /k/, not /kuh/ |
| d | duck or dog | /d/, not /duh/ |
| f | fish | /f/, not /fuh/ |
| g | goat or gate | /g/, not /guh/ |
| h | house or hat | /h/, not /huh/ |
| j | jam or jello | /j/, not /juh/ |
| k | kite or king | /k/, not /kuh/ |
| l | lion or lamp | /l/, not /luh/ This sound can be felt if prolonged until the throat opens on the *i* sound, as in *lion*. |
| m | mother or mittens | /m/ The lips stay closed. |
| n | nest or nuts or nurse | /n/, not /nuh/ |
| p | pig or paint | /p/, not /puh/ |
| qu | queen | /kw/, not /kwuh/ |
| r | rug or rose or rooster | /r/, not /ruh/ or /er/ This letter can be felt by prolonging its sound before opening the throat on the long *o* sound, as in *rose*. |
| s | sun | /s/ (Sometimes /z/, as in boys) |
| t | turtle or turkey or table | /t/, not /tuh/ |

*CONSONANTS, cont'd*

| Letter | Key Word | Something about the sound to be taught |
|--------|----------|----------------------------------------|
| v | vase or valentine | /v/, not /vuh/ Start to say *vase,* but stop before the long vowel *a* sound is made, and the correct sound of the *v* will be heard and felt. |
| w | wagon or watch | /w/, not /wuh/ Instead of saying *wagon,* say *agon,* and, by the omission of the *w*, its sound can be heard and felt. |
| x | bo*x* | /ks/, not /ex/ In our language the *x* is not found at the beginning of words. |
| y | yarn or yellow | /y/, not /yuh/ Instead of saying *yarn,* say *arn,* and by the omission of the *y* its sound and feel can be perceived. |
| z | zebra | /z/, not /zuh/ |

First graders soon learn that the consonant *s* can have the sound of the *z* also, as in wa*s*.

They learn that *q* is always followed by *u* in our language so *qu* is taught as a "unit."

Children are taught that *c, k,* and *ck* all have the same sound . . . /k/. The *ck* is the first consonant digraph they learn, and that it is never found at the beginning of a word in our language.

No other consonant digraph is taught until the letters that make the digraph "unit" have been learned. Then they learn the following:

| | |
|--|--|
| sh — ship | wh — wheel |
| th — this | In making the *wh* sound, only air can be felt on the hand held before |
| ch — chair | the mouth. The throat does not touch when this sound "blows out." |
| th — thimble | It is unlike the *w* sound which does not produce any air on the hand held before the mouth. |

23

## Small Manuscript Alphabet Cards

Approximate Size — 3" x 4". This to be determined by depth of pocket in the Chart Holder.

Two sets of the Small Manuscript Alphabet Cards are recommended. They can be purchased.* (Refer to pages 25 and 49.)

If the cards are made by the teacher, care must be taken to use heavy black strokes, approximately 1/8 to 1/4 inch, enabling them to be seen easily by a child in any part of the room. Letters should be in manuscript. Letters should be placed on the corresponding writing line of each card to insure their appearance on the same line when arranged to form words. Also, letters having stems that go below the line must not disappear into the pocket of the Chart Holder.**

In addition to the Small Manuscript Alphabet Cards for use in the Chart Holder, teachers often make a larger set about 5" x 7" for their own personal use when giving class drill. (Refer to page 154.)

The Small Manuscript Alphabet Cards will be handled by both the teacher and the children when making words on the Chart Holder or while learning them as "single units."

On the Chart Holder the Alphabet Cards are always kept *in alphabetical order*.

*Consonants*, consonant digraphs and letter combinations are made on *light colored tagboard*—cream or white.

*Vowels*, vowel digraphs, dipthongs and phonograms that "open the *throat*" are made on *salmon colored cards*.

*Beth H. Slingerland, *Small Manuscript Alphabet Cards*, Cambridge, Mass., Educators Publishing Service, Inc., 1971, 1974.
**Chart Holder refers to the word and phrase card holders that can be purchased from Educators Publishing Service, Cambridge, Mass.

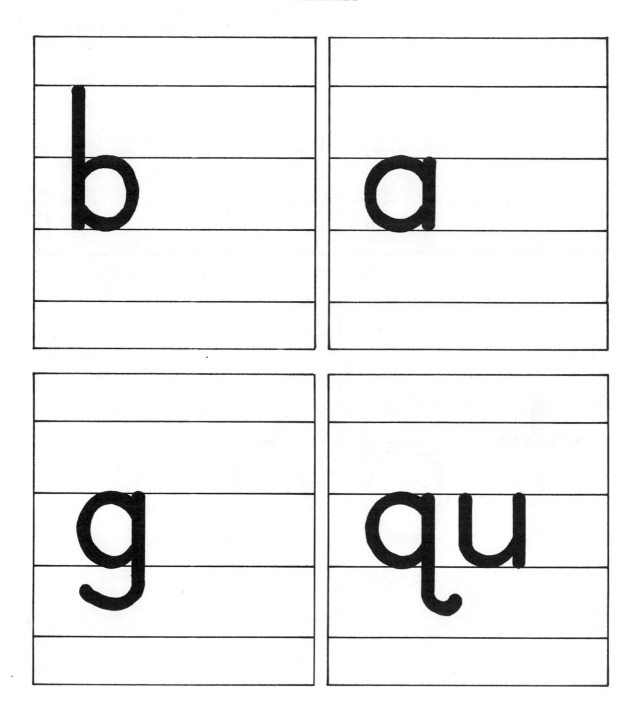

By writing the letters near the left hand edge of the cards they can be overlapped when arranged into words. This keeps letters close together in such a way that the completed word *looks like a word* and not like letters strung out along a line. (Refer to pages 82 and 163.)

CHART HOLDER POCKET

# tag

CHART HOLDER POCKET

The *key words* should be written on the backs of the Alphabet Cards for quick and easy reference by the teacher. The same key words are used on both the Manuscript Alphabet Cards and the Wall Cards, but only the Wall Cards have pictures to serve as cues for the sounds. (Refer to pages 19, 20, & 21.)

EXAMPLES

| | |
|---|---|
| a | a/ă/ apple |
| front | back |
| i | i/ĭ/ Indian |
| front | back |
| qu | qu/kw/ queen |
| s | s/s/sun /z/is |
| ow | ow/ō/snow /ou/cow |
| ar | ar/är/car |
| ing | ing/ĭng/ sing |
| ank | ank/ăngk/ bank |

letter combinations

27

Directions for making the Small Manuscript Cards including more-than-one-letter "units" of sight and sound are given below.

The following cards are used with *first year children* and *with children in any grade being introduced to SLD instruction for the first time.*

## WITH BEGINNERS

*Light Colored Cards*

*All consonants* to have the same key words as shown by pictures on the Wall Cards. (Refer to pages 19, 20, & 21.)

### Consonant Digraphs

ck – jack
sh – ship
ch – chair
wh – wheel
th – thimble /th/ *th*is

### Letter Combinations

ing – sing /ing/

*Salmon Colored Cards*

The *vowels* a, e, i, o, u to have the same key words as shown by pictures on the Wall Cards. (Refer to page 31.)

### Vowel Digraphs

ee – feet /ē/
oo – moon /o͞o/
    book /o͝o/

### Diphthongs

ou – ouch /ou/

### Phonograms

ar – star /är/
er – her /ûr/

## SECOND YEAR

The following "units" of sight and sound are added to the First Year Alphabet Card Pack for *second year* children and for *older children following a continuum of instruction.*

*Light Colored Cards*

*Syllable "units"* such as:

| | | |
|---|---|---|
| tion | – dictation | /shŭn/ |
| sion | – mission | /shŭn/ |
| | vision | /zhŭn/ |
| ple | – purple | /p'l/ |
| tle | – little | /t'l/ |

*Salmon Colored Cards*

| | | | |
|---|---|---|---|
| y as a vowel | – | gym | -/ĭ/ |
| | – | my | -/ī/ |
| | – | baby | -/ē/ |
| ay | – | play | /ā/ |
| ai | – | rain | /ā/ |
| aw | – | saw | /ô/ |
| au | – | Paul | /ô/ |

*Consonant Digraphs*

| | | | |
|---|---|---|---|
| ph | — | phone | /f/ |
| kn | — | knife | /n/ |

*Letter Combinations*

| | | | |
|---|---|---|---|
| ang | — | sang | /ang/ |
| ink | — | sink | /ingk/ |
| ank | — | sank | /angk/ |

| | | | |
|---|---|---|---|
| ea | — | eat | /ē/ |
| | | head | /ĕ/ |
| | | steak | /ā/ |
| ew | — | few | /ū/ |
| | | blew | /o͞o/ |
| eigh | — | sl*eigh* | /ā/ |
| or | — | c*or*n | /ôr/ |
| ir | — | b*ir*d | /ûr/ |
| ur | — | b*ur*n | /ûr/ |
| a-e | — | s*a*f*e* | /ā/ |
| e-e | — | th*ese* | /ē/ |
| i-e | — | d*i*m*e* | /ī/ |
| o-e | — | h*o*m*e* | /ō/ |
| u-e | — | m*u*l*e* | /ū/ |
| | | fl*u*t*e* | /o͞o/ |
| igh | — | n*igh*t | /ī/ |
| ie | — | pie | /ī/ |
| | | chief | /ē/ |
| oa | — | boat | /ō/ |
| oi | — | oil | /oi/ |
| oy | — | boy | /oi/ |
| ow | — | snow | /ō/ |
| | | cow | /ou/ |

The same Manuscript Alphabet Cards are used in the third and fourth years or as a continuum to what already has been learned. To the pack of already learned cards can be added:

*Salmon Colored Cards*

| | rain | | night | | star |
|---|---|---|---|---|---|
| ai | rain | igh | night | ar | star |
| ay | play | ie | pie | or | corn |
| aw | saw | ie | chief | er | her |
| au | Paul | | | ir | bird |
| | | | | ur | burn |
| ee | feet | oa | boat | | |
| ea | eat | oi | oil | | |
| ea | head | oy | boy | a-e | safe |
| ea | steak | ou | ouch | i-e | pine |
| ew | few | ow | cow | o-e | home |
| ew | blew | ow | snow | u-e | cube |
| eigh | sleigh | oo | moon | e-e | these |
| | | oo | book | | |

eu     — Europe    /ū/

ei     — vein    /ā/
      leisure    /ē/

Pronunciation of ey    — they    /ā/
depends upon which    — turkey    /ĭ/
dictionary is used    — turkey    /ē/

ie     — mischief    /ĭ/

When the third sound of the *ie*, which was introduced in the second year, is included, no new card needs to be made. Just another sound for *ie* has to be learned.

ui     — fruit    /o͞o/
      suit    /ū/

ue     — rescue    /ū/
      true    /o͞o/

(Reference has been made to old and new Webster's Dictionaries. Diacritical marks are from the old dictionary.)

When children have mastered these cards, reference to *Remedial Training for Children with Specific Disability in Reading, Spelling and Penmanship,* Gillingham and Stillman, Cambridge, Mass., Educators Publishing Service, Inc., 1956 or 1960 is recommended.

On tagboard 24" x 36" charts, such as those shown below, are made. They are placed where children can refer to them throughout the year.

By Summer School Teachers

**Patterns for Tracing**[*]

Each letter of the alphabet—one for each child—is made on separate sheets. These letter patterns are kept as *permanent patterns* on which the children make no marks, using their first two fingers only, for tracing. The teacher keeps them on the shelf, giving to children only the ones that are to be learned or practiced during a lesson. Following practice they are collected and stored for future use. (Refer to page 45.)

Each lower case letter should be made 8 to 10 inches high in heavy black strokes. Relative size is disregarded with beginners at first, the purpose being to "fix," for automatic recall, the gross motor movement of each form.

Some schools have the teacher's original patterns reproduced in quantity on school reproducing equipment—a set for each child. Patterns can be used for more than one year.

## EXAMPLES

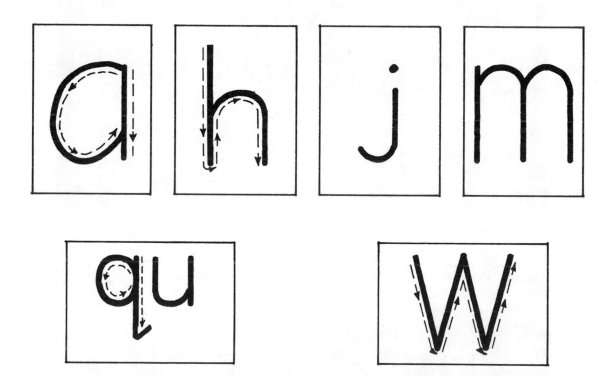

*Sets of permanent patterns for each child may be purchased: *Patterns for Tracing Letters of the Alphabet,* Cambridge, Mass., Educators Publishing Service, Inc., 1971.

**Expendable Patterns for Each Child**

After each new letter has been introduced, and while it is being learned, patterns, such as that illustrated below, are made before a lesson begins—one for each child. The patterns are for:

Tracing
Copying
Writing from Memory

To be made on 12 x 18 inch newsprint. (Refer to page 46.)

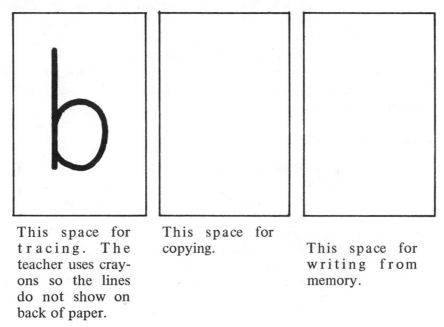

This space for tracing. The teacher uses crayons so the lines do not show on back of paper.

This space for copying.

This space for writing from memory.

The teacher uses crayons to prevent the lines from showing through the paper. When folded as shown below, the third space can be used for *writing from memory*. Other letters already taught can be practiced in the spaces on the back of the paper.

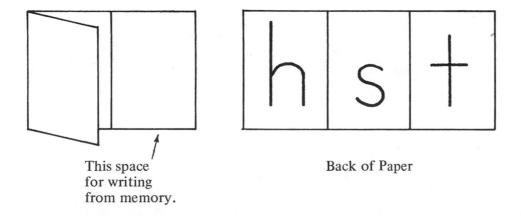

This space for writing from memory.

Back of Paper

33

**Classroom Equipment and Material:**

Blackboards

Chart Holder - Regular commercial Chart Holders for word and phrase cards used in teaching reading. Most primary classrooms are equipped with them.

Primary pencils without erasers.

12 x 18 inch newsprint.

1 inch lined composition paper for use after writing of letters and words has been introduced.

One half inch lined composition paper for writing when the size of letters is to be reduced.

Felt pens that make black strokes from 1/8 to 1/4 inch in order that children can see prepared material from any place in the room.

Crayons for teacher-made expendable patterns.

Very useful are:        Consonant Pictures for Peg Board
No. 272-1
Ideal School Supply Company, Chicago, Illinois

Reading Material -      Any basic readers such as:
Bank Street
Scott-Foresman
Houghton Mifflin
Ginn, etc.

Simple reading material for children's selection may be found in library books.

"Programmed" reading material *is not recommended* for use when following instruction in the Specific Language Disability technique presented herein.

## PART 3

TEACHING PROCEDURES
AUDITORY APPROACH AND
LEARNING TO WRITE FOR
SPELLING AND WRITTEN EXPRESSION

# A MULTI-SENSORY APPROACH

## Procedures With S.L.D. First Year Beginners

Instruction is started with the introduction of single letters of the alphabet. Because language depends on the automatic association of the visual-auditory-kinesthetic records perceived and stored on the brain and because Specific Language Disability children, for whatever the reason, fall short of this necessary interneurological organization, appropriate preventive measures from the outset for first graders identified as showing weaknesses in this perceptual-associational functioning are possible and advisable. All three linkages are used to develop spontaneous association:

1. The *auditory-kinesthetic* when the initial stimulus is *visual.*

2. The *visual-kinesthetic* when the initial stimulus is *auditory.*

3. The *visual-auditory* when the initial stimulus is *kinesthetic.*

*Instructional Time Blocks for Each Approach*

A special time block is arranged for *Learning to Write* in which letter *forms,* their *names,* and their *sounds* are taught — *leading into their use in the Auditory Approach.*

The AUDITORY APPROACH begins as soon as several letters are learned, and *blending* (encoding), as the initial step toward *spelling and written work* can be started. These procedures will be given on the *white pages.*

The VISUAL APPROACH is devoted to *reading* (decoding). These procedures are found on the *green pages.*

The Specific Language Disability teacher should plan the instructional work to fit into the arrangement of time blocks for the different approaches as shown below:

| 1. Learning to Write (white pages) | |
| --- | --- |
| 2. Auditory Approach (as shown on white pages) | 3. Visual Approach (as shown on green pages) |

Early identification of children whose screening gives indication of some possible difficulty in learning to read need *not mean* that reading should be delayed until they have been taught to unlock phonetic words, nor is this necessarily recommended. The introduction to reading begins at the same time it does in any regular classroom of Non-SLD children. Each group of children within the classroom receives its own individualized "preventive" SLD instruction, geared to its own rate of intake, integration and output. Only the instructional technique differs from that for Non-disability children.

At this early stage in development, children *have not failed* and are subject to "patterning" as a preventive measure to afford success in early academic experiences. Some SLD groups, just as with non-SLD groups, are able to progress more rapidly than others.

Reading, as a Visual Approach, can begin and be taught concurrently with Learning to Write and to spell, as presented in the Auditory Approach. (Refer to page 39.) Refer to the VISUAL APPROACH ON THE GREEN PAGES, 153 on.

Teaching within the separate approaches over a period of several years leads to the *ultimate goals* — which are *functional performances* in all areas of language.

By beginning early with children before failure occurs, the instruction can be considered *preventive* rather than corrective or remedial. However, the same plan for approaching the instructional techniques is applicable to those identified after failure sets them apart.

Procedures within each approach will be explained as this "Guide" is followed.

## ORGANIZATION WITHIN WHICH SPECIFIC LANGUAGE DISABILITY TECHNIQUES ARE PRESENTED

Circles and lines indicate goals for 1st year

LEARNING TO WRITE which leads into the Auditory Approach

### AUDITORY APPROACH

**A.** *Alphabet Cards*
Letter sounds are given.
(Refer to pages 53-54.)

**B.** *Blending* (Encoding)
(Refer to pages 77—)

**C.** *Spelling*
1. Phonetic — "Green Flag"
2. Non-Phonetic — "Red Flag"
   or to be "learned"
3. Ambiguous — "Yellow Flag"
4. Suffixes — Phrases — Sentences

**D.** *Dictation*
Phrases — Sentences —
Paragraphs —
Second year continuum
Punctuation

### VISUAL APPROACH

**A.** *Alphabet Cards*
Letters are exposed.
(Refer to pages 52-53.)

**B.** *Unlocking Words* (Decoding)
(Refer to bottom of page 84.)

**C.** *Reading Preparation* of specific
material, using SLD technique.
Four steps (Refer to page 175.)
1.
2.
3.
4.

**D.** *Reading* the prepared material
with structured guidance in
phrasing, concept, word attack,
rhythm and how to study.
(Refer to pages 185 — )

### THE GOAL

**E.** *Propositional and Creative Writing*
(Refer to page 144 and to
*Independent Creative Ideas For Use
with SLD children.)**

**E.** *Independent Reading*
At first — below instructional
level and eventually — anything

*Eldra O'Neal, and Helen Zylstra, *Independent Creative Ideas for Use with SLD Children,* Cambridge, Mass., Educators Publishing Service, Inc., 1971.

## LEARNING TO WRITE LETTERS OF THE ALPHABET

Instruction begins with each letter of the alphabet being taught as a "single unit" of sight and sound and "feel." As each letter is introduced its *wall card* (page 19) is placed on the wall, usually above the chalk boards, to be left throughout the year for easy reference of the children. They always are placed in alphabetical order with spaces left unfilled for the letters yet to be taught and then pinned in their correct relationship to the others. However, when about fifteen have been learned, all can be put on the wall because, by then, the pattern of learning should be well established and understood by the children. The teacher continues to teach each letter even if it has been placed on the wall.

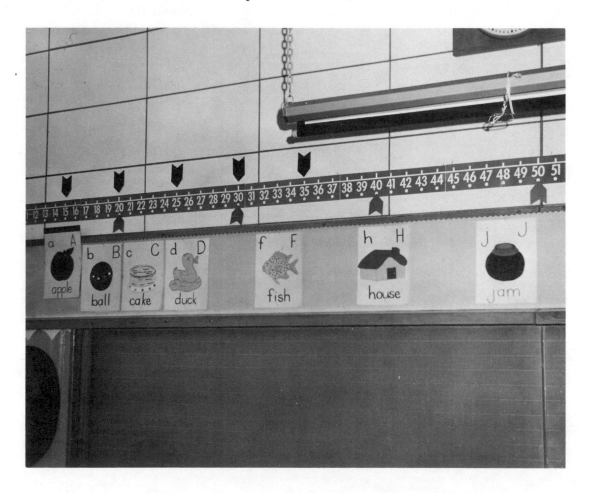

By Cheery Howse

The order for introducing letters is arbitrary and they do not have to be presented in alphabetical order . . *nor is this recommended* . . their needs in functional use determining their introduction.

Experience of trained Specific Language Disability teachers has shown that usually eight to ten letters can be learned and put into functional use by the beginning of the new year, assuming the work begins in September. The general maturity and readiness of the group also must be considered.

A suggested list of letters to be taught during the first three or four months is as follows:

h - s - l - b - t and the vowel a
m - k - c - f - g and the consonant digraph ck

By Betty Stuntz

## STRUCTURING A NEW LEARNING
### Consonants as Letters of the Alphabet

Structuring this new learning begins with discussion of what letters are — how they make words and the names of people, and of how words can make stories or give messages to people.

The consonant "h" serves as a good beginning letter. (The "b" and the "d" require special teaching for which reason their introduction should be left for a future time.) The sequential steps to follow require a period of several days.

**The First Step:** The *wall card* is held before the children, the teacher placing her hand below the lower case "h" and telling the children its *name.* Individual children, and *not the group speaking in unison,* are asked to pronounce "h" as the teacher continues to hold her hand under the letter.

Some children with Specific Language Disability are unable to remember the names of objects (anomia) even when there is concept. It is important to have them *hear* the teacher pronounce a word correctly and then to *repeat* while looking at the letter. This is done to reinforce the visual, auditory and kinesthetic linkages and integrative process with concept. For the teacher to name a letter of the alphabet is not enough. The child must repeat in order to *hear* his own voice and to *feel* the movement in his speech mechanism while *seeing* the symbol or symbols.

**The Second Step**: The teacher then forms a large "h" on the blackboard making it at least 12" to 15" tall and *naming* it as it is being formed. (Use a thick side of the chalk so the strokes can be seen easily by all the children.)

One at a time, children are asked to trace several times over a pattern made on the blackboard (a new pattern for each child). They should use full swings from the shoulders while naming the letter as it is being formed.

To prevent any tense or perfection-seeking child from *drawing* the letter, the teacher holds the child's hand, guiding the arm in a full swinging motion for the gross sequential movement pattern to be *felt by the child* before dependence upon self-direction of the movement is required. Some will have no difficulty, but others will have a great deal of kinesthetic-motor weakness. Such help may have to be given frequently over a period of time to the same child, or children, not necessarily because there is lack of effort, but rather because difficulty in recall of sequential movements involved is part of the disability.

*"Talk" the child, or children, into recalling and performing* by saying: "h — down all the way — up and around — down." This patterns thought which, in these children, must direct the kinesthetic-motor movement before automatic recall is established.

The teacher must "over-teach" and not assume that all children should have learned because some have.

**The Third Step**: Make several patterns on the blackboard so several children can trace at one time, *naming the letter each time it is formed,* while the other children name and trace in the air. The teacher should be actively alert to individual need of assistance or reinforcement.

Whenever possible, *prevent* rather than allow mistakes to be made; i.e., beginning a stroke from the bottom and going upward when it should begin at the top and go downward. During this time the teacher helps the child in need, explaining, making new patterns, guiding the insecure arm movement and sometimes discussing difficulties with the whole class.

Have the children who are watching form the "h" in the air, using arms in a swinging motion. The arms are extended with the elbows comfortably bent, the hands about at the same level as the top of the head to allow for the downward stroke of the tall letters and at eye level for the shorter letters. This allows for easy swings from the shoulder blades.

The two first fingers held together are used in place of a pencil.

The letter "h" is carried over the three sensory channels when the child *sees* the "h" (Visual), *hears* its name while it is pronounced (Auditory), and *feels* the sequential movement in the speech mechanism while pronouncing the "h", and *feels* the sequential movement pattern while forming the letter with the arm (Kinesthetic) — a multi-sensory approach, all building toward the simultaneous association and integration of sight, sound, and "feel." This is necessary to secure automatic recall.

The teacher must never forget that the majority of *non-Specific Language Disability* children can perceive a given language stimulus, such as the "h" over any one of the three sensory channels — auditory, visual, kinesthetic — and instantly associate or match it with the other two. Such non-disability children can do, *without conscious effort,* what children with various degrees of Specific Language Disability must put forth *conscious effort to learn to do.* SLD children have much insecurity of memory. What Dr. Dale Bryant points out as desirable remedial instruction is equally useful for initial preventive instruction. "Remediation should focus on the simplest, most basic perceptual-associational elements in reading; perception of details within the gestalt of words and association of sound with the perceived word elements . . . . Perceptual and associational *responses should be overlearned until they are automatic."*

In the technique to follow it is necessary to structure a pattern of intake in such a way that all three sensory channels are linked in automatic association upon perception of the initial stimulus which must include integration and storage for recall when needed. Without secure recall, modalities of output cannot carry correct impulses for successful performance in the language area.

Good SLD teachers must put conscious effort into structuring each new step that requires a new learning for SLD children. To rush or to try to hurdle intervening steps in an attempt to keep up with regular classes of non-SLD boys and girls, or to think that following a curriculum is more important than following children's individual rates of intake, is confusing, frustrating and discouraging to them in their initial efforts to learn to do what the majority accomplish readily.

The children gain momentum as they *learn how to learn.*

To provide *motivation is not the problem.* These children provide this for themselves with their first recognition of success.

Experience shows teachers how to group children within a classroom so that particular needs can be emphasized and reinforced.

**The Fourth Step:** Teachers find that it takes from one to three days to reach this fourth step.

Previously prepared *permanent patterns for tracing* are given to each child. (Refer to page 32.)

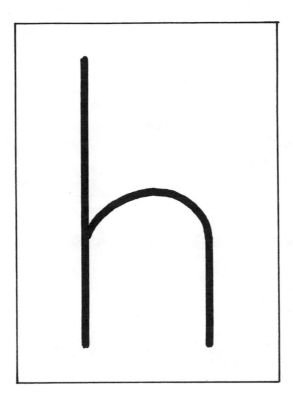

Different school systems have prepared the letters to be run off on reproducing equipment enabling the making of a set for each child. The teacher needs to make only the one original set for copy. They can be run off on 12 x 18 inch newsprint or on any size down to 9 x 12 inch paper.

The children are directed to use *the first two fingers* in place of a pencil for tracing over the pattern of the "h" and to use a swinging arm movement from the shoulder as the *letter is named.* Do not allow them to use "drawing" strokes over the pattern or the sequential movement required to form the "h" will be lost.

The purpose of tracing is to instill the gross movement for instant recall. This cannot be done through a drawing motion or the purpose of tracing will be missed. Refinement comes through the fingers after the sequential movement pattern is thoroughly "fixed" and automatic.

When the children can move their arms freely in tracing they are ready to use the *unsharpened* ends of their pencils.

**The Fifth Step**: On the same *permanent patterns* have the children trace over the "h" with the *unsharpened* end of their primary pencils, *always naming the letter as it is traced*.

This is the time to see that children *know how to grasp the pencils*, to sit correctly with knees together and to place papers in good position.

Desks should be cleared of everything but the papers on which to trace.

This affords an early opportunity to show how to handle school working materials.

Collect the *permanent patterns* for future use.

**The Sixth Step**: *Patterns made by the teacher for tracing and copying* are distributed, possibly on another day. (Refer to page 33.)

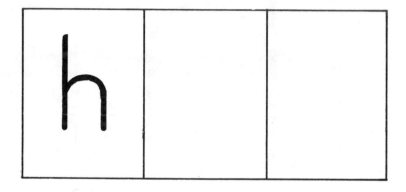

This lesson begins with *tracing* — a review of what has been practiced on previous days.

To use the *writing end of the pencil* will be a step toward independent writing.

To *copy* will require guidance and supervision by the teacher.

Following a brief review, have the pencils held in readiness for using the sharpened end. Impress on the children the need to have fingers hold where the color of the pencil ends and the sharpened part begins. They should not let their fingers touch the lead or the tip. They *trace lightly* over the pattern (as they already have been taught to do before making an actual mark) letting the arm swing from the shoulder and *naming the letter as it is formed, not after, and not before*.

Discourage pressing heavily because patterns will become distorted with dark lines that cover the teacher's letter forms. Lines that are too heavy usually indicate tenseness or insecure memory of the letter form which calls for more teacher help. The teacher holds the child's arm at the wrist, having him relax to enable his perception of the feeling of the guided movement.

The children continue to *trace* lightly over this *one* pattern until the teacher sees they are *ready to copy*.

*Copying* begins following teacher judgment of children's readiness. The children are directed to make the letter "h" by themselves in the next space.

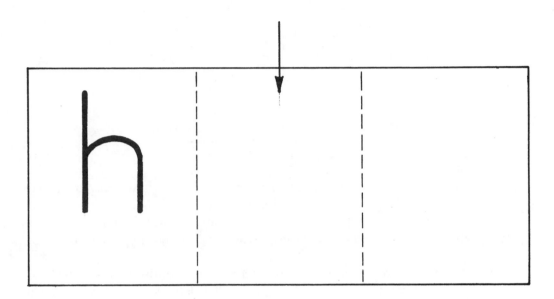

Sometimes children are encouraged to try first with the unsharpened end of the pencil to be sure of placement in the space, and to be sure they can remember the "feel" of the "h."

Show how to begin below the top edge of the paper and to stop before reaching the bottom edge. Otherwise the marks get on the desk. Also, using a book to illustrate, point out marginal arrangement on the pages to make this concept clear.

Children who make reasonably good copies can *trace over their own patterns*.

For those having difficulty, the teacher reinforces their lines with red crayon or markers so children will trace over accurately made patterns.

Over a period of days, and sometimes longer, with much tracing and copying, writing ability and recall improve and become automatic. During this time of learning, *do not waste time by asking a child where he could have improved a letter form*. Instead, *show him* by marking over the lines needing improvement with a colored pencil or crayon or by guiding the child's arm in forming a letter.

*Use of erasers* is discouraged from the beginning. Encourage *thought before* action. When a mistake is made, have the child disregard it by tracing over the pattern as it should be. Point out that the papers are "*practice papers*" for learning.

*Writing from Memory* — Have the children fold the tracing space of their papers over the copying space. This covers up all their work. They are ready to write from memory on the last, unused space.

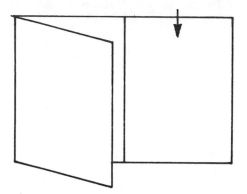

Have the children make the letter "h" from memory. If right, they may trace over their own patterns. They can refer to what was previously done on the first two spaces.

The spaces on the back of the page can be used in the same way. After more letters have been learned these spaces can be used to review already learned letters. (Refer to page 33.)

Teachers of SLD children need to remember that some children are able to make well formed letters when they are *seen,* but may fail later when unable to recall their appearance when *not seen,* or to associate them with their names when *heard.* To strengthen this language requirement children should:

Trace — to acquire the sequence of movement.

Name the Letter — while tracing to associate the name as it is heard and the "feel" in speech and in the arm.

See the Letter — to associate the *visual* symbol with the *sound* of its name, and the way it *feels* in speech and in writing.

The weakest sensory channel, whichever it may be, is associated with the strongest in this way. Until the three are linked, recall may be lost or confused. Modalities of output for reading, writing, and spelling, and oral and written expression depend on recalls of previous intake — perception, integration, concept, all associated and stored for instant recall.

*Functional writing, or penmanship, needs to become an automatic response so conscious thought can be directed toward what is to be expressed in words and not toward how the letters are formed.* (Refer to page 39.)

*All the letters* are taught by *tracing, copying,* and eventually practice in writing from *memory,* following the steps as given above.

## A — ALPHABET CARDS

**Structuring a New Learning** — The Sound a Letter Makes in Association with its Visual Symbol and its Kinesthetic-Motor Pattern.

As soon as the children have learned the "h" reasonably well, the *sound it makes* is taught. Teacher judgment must determine how soon after the preceding steps this should be.

Discussion precedes the teaching. The letters make sounds and the sounds when put together in different ways make words. After the names of the letters and their sounds are learned, children will be able to use them for spelling and to "unlock" unrecognized phonetic words for reading.

First, the teacher points to the "h" on the wall card and says:

"H makes the sound that can be *heard and felt* at the beginning of the name of this picture — *house* — /h/."

"We tell about the *h* like this: *h* — house, /h/."

The *h* is named, the key word *house* is named, and the sound /h/ is given so the children *hear the teacher.*

While it is desirable for teachers to use well modulated voices, it is equally desirable for children to hear what the teacher is saying. Also, in the beginning, they need *to see* the teacher to make the sound and *to hear* that the sound /h/, for example, is made with air alone and not with voices, by letting the walls of the throat touch. After the first lesson or two, they should depend upon their own ears and not on watching the teacher form the sound.

(NOT INCLUDED ARE GAMES AND DEVICES FOR HEARING THE LETTER SOUND IN OTHER WORDS, BUT THEY ARE HIGHLY RECOMMENDED.)

*Next,* call upon individual children to:

1. *Name* the letter, at the same time forming it in the air with the arm.

2. *Name* the key word picture.

3. *Give the sound* that the letter makes. (Give immediate help if a child makes the sound incorrectly. Help the child to *hear and feel* the sound when the key word is repeated. The teacher may need to over emphasize its sound as the key word is pronounced.)

The *key word picture,* as an easily recognized *object of constant form,* serves as the cue to recall.

*Individual* children, and *not the class in unison,* "tell about the *h*"; otherwise the teacher may fail to hear the child who makes errors or says nothing at all. *Such children need*

49

*preventive help at the moment and not corrective help at some later date when the wrong impressions have become implanted on the brain.*

Often children with weak auditory and kinesthetic perception or associations or recall can be detected at this time by an alert teacher.

*If the teacher* is not sure of the correct sounds of the letters of the alphabet, this is the time to recheck or to seek help. Reference to the Childs Phonetic Records is recommended. (Refer to pages 18, 21-23.)

*In the third step* have individual children (while the others watch) go to the blackboard, make an "h" and tell about it as follows:

1. Name the  *h*  as it is formed, *speaking loud enough to be heard* and to feel their own speech mechanism at work.

2. Name the key word — *"house"* — after the letter is formed.

3. Give the sound /h/.

Guide a child's *thinking* with as few words as possible on the part of the teacher. The more the teacher talks, the more cluttered becomes the child's pattern of *thinking through the several steps for himself.*

Say, if help is needed: "Name the letter; name the key word; give the sound." Perhaps a child may need only one of the three cues.

Perhaps all three cues might be needed to reinforce the three sequential steps, but when the teacher tells the child to "think hard so you can remember what the *sound* is" *too many words break up the thought pattern.* The child needs to learn to "think through the sequential steps" for himself with *only enough help to trigger thought for self-direction.*

The object is to get the children to perform in an automatic way without prompting so there will be simultaneous use of the three sensory pathways. The key words serve as cues for associating the graphic symbol and its "feel" with the auditory sound symbol.

The *wall card* is pinned up on the wall in its permanent place at this time.
The small *alphabet card* (pages 24-25) is placed in the Chart Holder.

From now on children are encouraged to look at the wall card if unsure of recall. Tell them to *look before making a mistake.* Eventually this "crutch" will not be needed and they, themselves, discard it when automatic recall becomes stable. However, no child is to be denied this reference point as long as needed. In time he can be urged to *think* before looking, but to look if recall is slow in coming.

If some child cannot remember the *name of a letter,* tell him to keep making the letter form with his arm "because your moving arm may tell you." If this fails, show the child where the letter name begins in the speech organs; e.g., *h* requires two sounds in its pronunciation — *a* and *ch.* Point to the throat where the long sound of the *a* is made and then to the forward part of the mouth where the *ch* sound is formed. Sometimes recall for the child who forgets can be triggered when the teacher simply places the thumb on the throat and the forefinger to the mouth. If this still does not work, tell the child to start making the letter *h* with the arm swing again and to say *a* and then point to the mouth. Usually with the help of several different ways of association, possibly on several occasions, recall is sparked and the child has learned how to follow this thinking process independently. Such a "thought pattern" as this often paves the way of thinking when recall of some other letter may be difficult.

**Teaching More Consonants** — The name and sound at the same time.

The next three or four consonants are to be introduced following the same steps as already given. As each letter is taught, its *wall card* is placed on the wall in its correct alphabetical position, spaces for the untaught letters being left in readiness following their presentation. (Refer to page 40.)

After several letters have been taught so that the "pattern" of learning is understood, *both the name of the letter and its sound* can be presented at the same time. The teacher holds up the new *wall card* and says:

"The name of this letter is _____ and it says _____ ."

The children, taking turns, tell about the letter by giving its *name, key word* and *sound,* just as they already have learned to do.

**How to Practice for Recall** — When initiated in each one of the three sensory channels.

As soon as a letter is introduced the *small alphabet card* is placed in the Chart Holder. To give practice for automatic recall with simultaneous association of both sight and sound symbols and the sequential movement patterns in speech and arm, the teacher must have understanding of the sensory approaches to be described below. This is necessary before use of this multi-sensory technique can be meaningful. *Otherwise, one of the sensory approaches may be overlooked entirely or neglected, that one usually being the auditory.*

*The Visual Approach—*which leads to reading.

> In the *Visual Approach* a small *alphabet card is exposed,* this stimulus carried over the visual sensory pathway to the cortex of the brain. Children *see,* (perceive) the graphic symbol on the card, recognize its meaning as a letter of the alphabet, (cognition) associate the letter *seen* with its *name and sound* (auditory), and with the way it *feels* in speech and in arm when writing (kinesthetic). To strengthen or "fix" the linkage of these three channels, or pathways, there needs to be supervised drill and supervised practice.

*Procedure*

The *alphabet card is exposed.*

Individual children:

1. *Name the letter* seen on the card, *forming it in the air* with a free arm swing from the shoulder.

2. *Name the key word* — (a common object of *constant form* which affords a reliable cue for recall).

3. *Give the sound* of the letter.

The *visual symbol* as perceived is transposed into its *auditory symbol* and associated with its *written form* — a multi-sensory experience.

*The Auditory Approach* — which leads to both oral and written spelling.

In the *Auditory Approach nothing is shown to the children*; the stimulus is carried to the cortex of the brain over the auditory sensory channels. Children *hear the sound symbol* when it is given by the teacher, recognize it as the sound of a letter (cognition), inwardly transpose it to its graphic symbol (visual) and then to the "feel" of its form (kinesthetic) which triggers the motor area of the brain into the necessary bodily performance as the letter is formed in the air with the arm and in the speech mechanism for verbalizing.

*Procedure*

The *sound of the letter* is given by the teacher.

Individual children:

1. *Name* the letter just heard, *forming it in the air.*

2. *Name* the key word.

3. *Give the sound* — looking at the *key word* to help in the recall of *sound* and *feel,* if needed.

   The *auditory sound symbol,* as perceived, was inwardly transposed into its *visual symbol* and associated with its *written form* and *speech pattern* — a multi-sensory experience.

While young children are learning the letters and their sounds, the teacher should *give both the sound and the key word* to strengthen the association of letter symbol and its sound symbol with a key picture to serve as a reliable cue for recall.

It is important for children to speak out enabling them to *hear* their own voices and to *feel* their own speech. The teacher must bring this about, knowing it is *fear of failure* and not necessarily shyness that all too often is the reason for the too-soft or mumbling voices.

The teacher says:

"What says /s/ as in *sun*?" and the child answers:
"S (forming the letter in the air), *sun* /s/."

In time, after children are sure of the key word, the teacher should give only the sound. However, when a child hesitates, give encouragement to look up at the *wall card*, or name the key word for the child. The key word is a crutch to be used for as long as needed and then put aside after months of over-use. Prevent mistakes whenever possible because mistakes confuse secure recall. Help children to learn to *think before performing,* which means allowing enough time, free of pressure and by not giving his turn to someone else if he hesitates. Sometimes reteaching may be needed, but if at all possible, guide a child's thought toward completion of what is undertaken so success is experienced. All this takes longer in the beginning, but will enable SLD children to gain momentum and self-dependence and to escape the crippling effects of guessing or failure. *Guessing should never be encouraged* regardless of its recommended use in techniques that are successful with non-SLD children.

*The Kinesthetic Approach* — which leads to handwriting and all written work.

In the *Kinesthetic Approach* nothing is *seen* or *heard,* the stimulus carried over the kinesthetic sensory pathway. Children *feel* the sequential movement of the letter form when the teacher guides the arm in writing the letter on the black-board. They recognize what is felt as a letter of the alphabet (cognition), and inwardly match it with its visual symbol and auditory sound.

*Procedure*

Place before a child's face a piece of cardboard approximately 10" x 12" while he faces the blackboard. *The rest of the class watches. The child sees and hears nothing.* The teacher guides the child's arm to form a large letter of the alphabet, being sure the arm swings freely at the shoulder.

Turn the child away from the blackboard without allowing him to see what the hand made. The class sees but must not say anything while waiting for the child to:

1. Name the letter, forming it in the air.

2. Name the key word.

3. Give the sound of the letter.

Discussion brings out that the arm carried the message. The child "felt" the letter and then knew what it was. It was *not the eyes, not the ears,* but *the arm* that told what letter was felt.

Bring out the fact that those who watch can *see and feel,* but can *hear no sound.* Children come to comprehend the "*inner sound*" they matched with what they *saw and felt* — a multi-sensory experience.

More children will want turns and those watching like to see if the child having a turn "gets the message" through *feeling* without *seeing or hearing.*

If the child does not recognize the letter by its "feel," guide his arm in its movement pattern again for several times. This may bring about recall. If not, ask the child to show on the chart what letter his hand made, but do not let him see what was made on the blackboard. Sometimes children point without hesitation to the correct letter. This tells the teacher that while there may be kinesthetic-visual association, the linkage with the auditory — the name of the letter — has not been reliably established. The child needs to *trace* such a letter and *name it while tracing, not before and not after, but while tracing.*

Sometimes the sound of the letter can be recalled, but not the name. More tracing, copying and experience with recall are indicated for such a child.

## DAILY ORGANIZATION

### Initial Steps to be Followed Daily in the Three
### Approaches to Language Arts

*Learning to Write Approach*
Kinesthetic — Visual — Auditory

Continue to teach new letters as follows:
Tracing — Copying — Writing from Memory
Key Words
Practice — Under Supervision
Review of What Has Been Learned
(Refer to pages 42-49.)

| *Auditory Approach* | *Visual Approach* |
|---|---|
| A.  *Cards* (Refer to pages 53-54.)<br><br>The card is *not exposed* as *the teacher gives the sound* of the letter. Have an individual child *tell about the sound* that was heard. The child:<br><br>1. *Names* the letter and *forms it in the air.*<br>2. *Names* the key word.<br>3. Gives the *sound.*<br><br>*The teacher exposes the card and the class repeats.*<br><br>Go through the pack of cards which should contain only the letters that have been taught in the LEARNING TO WRITE APPROACH.<br><br>Give each child a turn, or as many as time allows, but it is *advisable for every child to perform as an individual.* | A.  *Cards* (Refer to page 52-53.)<br><br>*Expose* one of the already taught letter cards. Have an individual child "tell about the letter." The child:<br><br>1. *Names* the letter and *forms it in the air.*<br>2. *Names* the key word.<br>3. Gives the *sound* of the letter.<br><br>The *class repeats.*<br><br>Go through the pack of cards which should contain only the letters that have been taught in the LEARNING TO WRITE APPROACH.<br><br>Give each child a turn or as many as time allows. |

Cards — continued
    See following pages.

B.   *Blending*.
    Omit until after the
    vowel *a* is introduced.
    (Refer to pages 66
    and 77-103.)

C.   *Spelling*
    Omit for now. (Refer to
    page 103 and on.)

B.   *Unlocking*.
    Omit until Auditory

    Approach, B—Blending
    becomes functional.
    (Refer to bottom of
    pages 84 and 153.)

C.   *Reading* (Refer to the green
    pages — VISUAL APPROACH
    pages 153 and 175-185.)

D.   (Refer to pages 185-199.)

### Combining the Learning to Write Period
### with the Auditory Approach
### for
### Practice in Association

*Auditory Stimulus* — with visual-kinesthetic (gross movement) association.

Ask a child to stand before the Chart Holder on which the cards arc arranged in alphabetical order. Following the same procedure as already explained in the *Auditory Approach:* (Refer to pages 53-54.)

1. The teacher gives the *sound* of any one of the letters.

2. The child finds the card containing the visual symbol and sets it in another pocket clearly apart from the others.

3. The child then a. *names and forms the letter in the air;* b. *names* the key *word;* and c. *gives the sound.*

4. The class repeats.

5. Now the child goes to the blackboard where *he can no longer* (but the class can) see the card in the Chart Holder. The child stands far enough back from the blackboard to allow ample room for him to swing his arm without touching it while he "tells about" the letter before writing it on the blackboard.

    The teacher watches the arm formation of the letter to be sure it will be written correctly when the child writes it with chalk on the blackboard, thereby *preventing* any mistake, if possible.

    Continue with other letters in the same way.

In future lessons, after the procedures given above are well understood and can be followed readily, each child is given a sheet of 12" x 18" newsprint to be folded in half, or in thirds.

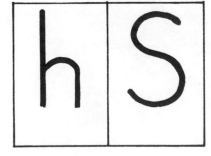 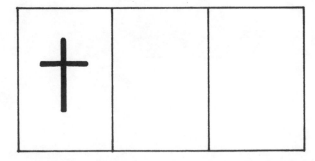

After the letter has been written on the blackboard, its good and poor points are noted, possibly giving the child another try, or having his arm guided by the teacher to reinforce the memory of its "feel."

The letter is erased. The card on the Chart Holder is covered.

All the children write the letter in the first space of their papers, naming it as it is being formed and then tracing over their own patterns. The teacher moves about to help and reassure as the children work.

Go through the whole procedure with another letter to be made in the next space. One child always performs first, and then the whole class writes.

The letter written on the blackboard by a child is erased and the card on the Chart Holder covered to stimulate recall and self-reliance by each individual child. Of course, if a child forgets he is encouraged to look up at the wall card rather than to guess. In time, children come to depend on themselves, but this point of reference should always be turned to if needed.

Make other letters on the back of the paper.

At this time do not attempt to teach relative size of the letters. The purpose is to develop automatic memory of the gross movement. Refinement comes later after the gross motor movement pattern of the letter is remembered. Then concentration can be placed on relative size and, eventually, the goal which is to use letters when spelling words.

*Practice to Develop Quick Recall of Letter Symbols from an Auditory Stimulus.*
As each new letter is taught during the time devoted to LEARNING TO WRITE, include it in all practice experiences.
Each child is given a sheet of 12" x 18" newsprint to be folded in thirds.

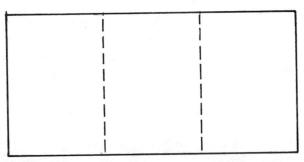

*The teacher names a letter.* A child is asked to:

1. Name and form the letter in the air.

2. Name the key word.

3. Give the sound.

(Be sure the child does not face the class when forming a letter or the children will see it in its reversed form.)

*The class* repeats, forming the letter in the air, using the large gross motor movement stemming from the shoulder.
The class writes the letter in the first space of the papers, each member tracing over his own pattern.
Continue in the same way with other letters.

On another day, the *teacher gives the sound* of a letter that has been learned and *a child*:

1. Names the letter, always forming it in the air.

2. Names the key word.

3. Gives the sound.

The class repeats the same procedure.

The children write the letter on their papers, tracing over their own patterns, *naming the letter softly, but clearly, as it is being traced.*

This insures an auditory — visual — kinesthetic association.

*A Kinesthetic Stimulus*

Using a kinesthetic stimulus, the teacher guides a child's hand in the formation of a letter on the blackboard (page 54) while the class watches. Without seeing what the hand wrote on the blackboard, although the class can see, the child goes to the Chart Holder and finds the letter that was *felt by the arm.*

The child tells about the letter in the usual way, already described.

The class repeats.

Sometimes *the class* can write the letter on its papers. Sometimes the class does not need to write on papers, but individual children can be given turns to *feel* each letter and then associate it with the visual symbol, *verbalizing* the experience.

### Teaching the *b* and *d* Requires Special Instruction

The *b* is taught first. At least eight to ten letters should be taught before the *d* is introduced.

The *b* is learned in one continuous stroke without lifting the arms.

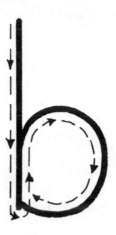

Learning the *b* is preceded with an auditory-motor activity before the permanent patterns are given to each child. The children are asked to stand, to put both arms straight out in front of themselves, and then they are told to:

"Swing your arms slowly out from your body until they are straight out from your shoulders."

When the children understand and can follow this body movement, have the left-handed children sit down until the teacher is ready to give them their turns. (It is wise to *name* the left-handed children because children are often confused about their handedness.)

Ask the right-handed boys and girls to hold out their *right* arms only — to *move them away from their bodies.* The teacher checks to see that all are able to follow the direction correctly.

Discussion brings out that this is the direction people follow when writing or reading.

Now the left-handed children are given their turns while the right-handed children watch. *Performance* and *discussion* brings out the fact that if left-handers move their arms "out from the body" they will not write in the direction handwriting is supposed to go. Therefore their arms must go *across the front of their bodies.*

Point out that nobody knows exactly why writing goes in this one particular direction; therefore, left-handed people have to tell themselves to move their arms "in front of my body" or "toward my other hand." Right-handers can say "go out from my body."

For learning the gross motor pattern of the *b*, follow the same procedure used with any letter, but point out which direction the round part of the *b* follows. Guide their thinking by saying:

"We start at the top and make the tall stem go all the way down. Now go up over the same line without lifting your arm, but *stop and think* which way the arm is going to go before making the round part."

Before children begin to write, it is sometimes helpful to have them make their arms go out from their bodies (or in front) in order to *feel* which way the round part of the *b* must go before they begin to write.

The teacher should demonstrate this performance on the blackboard, telling herself aloud what to do for all to see and hear her performance.

Remind the children that after they have learned to make any letter *their hands will do what their brains tell them to do if they take time to think first.*

The teacher *prevents* individuals from making mistakes if, when the critical point in a letter formation is reached, the child is told to "stop and think and show yourself which way to go" before completing its formation.

This is a *pattern of thinking* to help the child who is easily confused.

The *d* is learned by using an entirely different stroke from that of the *b*.

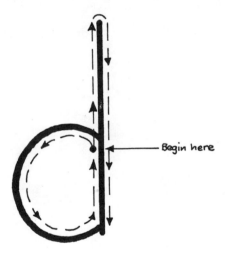

Begin here

Because the *"a"* is taught long before the *"d"* is presented, children can be given the auditory-motor experience of being told, and then telling themselves that "*d* goes round like an *a*." The teacher shows and guides the thinking by saying:

"Round like an *a* — tall stem — straight down to the line."

This is done with one continuous stroke without lifting the hand — unlike the line and circle used with non-SLD children.

Hearing the teacher and actually feeling their arms being guided through the movement pattern soon enables children to direct themselves. When the children practice, however, *they should name the letter at the same time it is being formed.*

Other letters that begin with the same stroke used in making an *a* are:

c　　g　　o　　qu　　s

With the *s* children tell themselves that it begins like an *a*.

With a g it goes "round like an *a*, straight down below the line, under and up."

The qu goes "round like an *a* , stem below the line, out from my body to the *u*."

**Preventing Number Symbol Confusion**

The 1 goes straight down.

The 2 goes "out from my body (or in front) and around."

The 3 goes "out from my body (or in front)."

The 4 goes "down, out from my body," all in one stroke and then "stem." (Left-handers go "down and in front of my body.")

The 5 goes "down, out from my body and around, top." (Left-handers, accordingly.)

The 6 goes "down, out from my body and around" in one continuous stroke. (Left-handers, as explained.)

The 7 goes "out from my body, straight down," all in one stroke.

The 8 goes: "Make an *s* , then go up" all in one continuous stroke.

The 9 goes "round like a little *a* , stem straight down," all in one stroke.

The 10 goes: "Make one ten *1* and no more *0* − 10."

Never hesitate to tell a child to *"stop and think,"* or, "stop and tell your hand what to do," when a critical point in either letter or number symbol orientation is reached. This is to help his *pattern of thought* in self-guidance become well established.

Pressure for speed *should be avoided.* Encourage *thought before guessing or plunging.* To build this thought and motor pattern in the beginning may take longer, but future performance brings rewards in secure self-reliance.

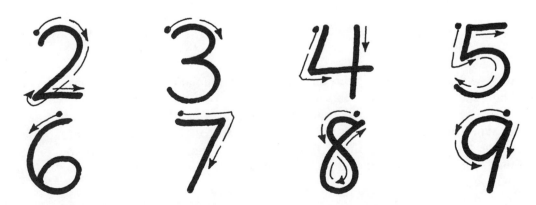

**Structuring a New Learning** — Vowels as Special Letters of the Alphabet

After three or four consonants have been learned, children are ready for a new learning — a vowel, with its short sound and its special purpose within words.

Only the vowel *a* is taught, with its short sound, before January (assuming the children start in September or October). Not until sometime in January is the second vowel *i* introduced. Then, another structured learning — discrimination — will be introduced.

> Before January children learn to use the consonants already taught to them with the one vowel *a* for blending single units of sound, (phonemes), into one-syllable phonetic words through the Auditory Approach. Until a *pattern of intake* is established this thought process must not be cluttered with too many learnings coming too fast to allow for securely organized thinking. Therefore, only one vowel is used until *vowel concept* is well comprehended, and blending is of functional use.

1. Teaching the vowel *a* begins with *discussion* to build concept.

Show the *wall card* and tell children that the letter *a* is called a vowel and that a vowel *sound* causes people to do something special every time a word is pronounced. Ask the children *to listen and to think* to see if they can discover the special reason for vowel sounds. The teacher says:

> "If I were to play ball with you I might tell you to get the ball while I get the *bt* . You get the ball while I get the *bt*."

Children will soon point out the teacher's mispronunciation of *bat*. The teacher agrees with them and asks what she failed to do that would have enabled her to say *bat* correctly. Some child will discover that *the throat must open* before the word can be spoken correctly, and understandably. Children may discover for themselves the short sound of the *a*, but the teacher tells and shows how the throat opens and has the children experiment with this *feeling* when they repeat words *named by* the teacher; e.g., *lag, tam, pad, rag, fat, sap, wham, ran, van, ham.*

This is the time for *vowel concept* to be understood. "Vowel sounds open our throats." Eventually, when diphthongs and vowel digraphs such as *ai* and *ee* , respectively, are learned, they will understand that some letters grouped together make the *vowel sound* and that every word in our language must have a vowel sound to allow all the sounds to blend together.

2. The *vowel a* wall card is held before the children, the teacher pointing to the *a* and saying:

"A – apple – /ă/" and then "A says /ă/ as in apple."

Next the teacher makes a large *a* (lower case, not a capital) on the blackboard, *naming it as the arm forms it.* Tell the children that *a's* begin with a little hook that *goes up –* and *around* and back to the hook – and then straight down, all in one stroke.

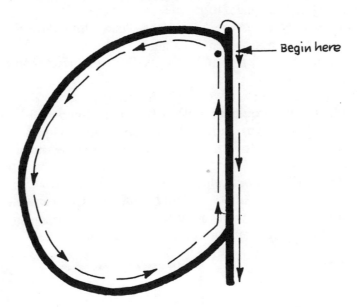

The children make the *a* in the air. (The teacher must be careful not to face the children when writing in the air, lest the letter be shown in its mirrored form.)

3. The vowel *a* is now taught exactly as the preceding consonants were taught, first using the *permanent patterns* for tracing to acquire the gross motor movement. Then they *trace, copy, write from memory.* (Refer to page 42.) When learned, the *small alphabet card* is placed in the Chart Holder in a separate pocket with the consonants already learned and included in all practice.

*Teachers – Note:*
No *unlocking* of words through the *Visual Approach* is attempted until children learn how to blend through the *Auditory Approach* in the lessons to follow.

SUMMARY
    Each letter is introduced with:

| | |
|---|---|
| Tracing | — Prepared Patterns |
| Copying | — Referring to Prepared Patterns |
| Writing from Memory | — The Kinesthetic Movement Pattern Associated with Sight and Sound |
| Practice | — Including review of every letter already taught, using the Visual and Auditory and sometimes the Kinesthetic Approaches. |

The *wall cards* showing letters as they are taught are put on the wall. The *vowel a wall card* is placed in a space prepared for vowels only, or by being raised or lowered an inch or two if placed with the consonants, or by putting a red border around the whole card — to set them apart.(Refer to page 40.)

The small *alphabet cards* are left in the Chart Holder for reference and for use when needed. Be sure each card is kept in alphabetical order; e.g., *b  h  l  m  t* and after more letters are presented, *b  c  f  g  h  k  l  m  s  t*, etc. (Refer to pages 80 and 163.)

It is advisable to have two of each *alphabet card.* Then, when one is to be returned, it can be quickly and easily matched and replaced by the children. In this way, the recall of each letter's relationship in space to other letters of the alphabet becomes automatic, a desirable skill for use throughout the years ahead.

*The vowel a small alphabet card* is placed in a separate row, apart from the consonants. It will have been made on a *salmon colored card,* or on a *cream colored card* (the same as the consonant cards) bordered with red or with one of the corners colored red to designate it as a vowel. (Refer to page 25 for correct letter placement.)

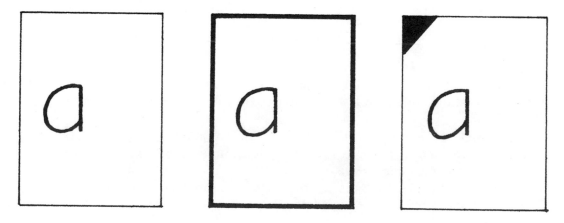

Usually by November, the consonants *h, l, m, b,* and the vowel *a* will have been taught in *preparation for the next step, which is blending for oral spelling* with use of the small alphabet cards to show the graphic "whole word" when the blending is completed — an auditory-visual association.

While learning to blend is being developed, *letter-size relationship which is the beginning of letter refinement in writing,* is introduced during the *Learning to Write* block of time. (Procedures given on pages to follow.)

*Letter-size relationship* is taught after the gross kinesthetic motor movement pattern of four or five letters has been learned to a satisfactory degree of automation. This *new learning* is taught during the *Learning to Write* period on the same days (and weeks) that *blending orally, using only such letters as have been taught,* is being developed in the Auditory Approach period with cards on the Pocket Chart.

*Written spelling is not attempted* until writing with correct letter-size relationship can be accomplished successfully by the children.

As soon as correct letter-size relationship is secure *and* children have learned how to blend, the two are combined in order for the goal — written spelling — to be successfully undertaken. The children will know how to form the letters and how to proceed when spelling a phonetic word. Concentration can be placed on how to *spell and write* words without losing sight of this goal by trying to recall letter form or how to follow sequential steps in blending.

**Structuring a New Learning** – Letter-size Relationship, Spacing, and Alignment
   This is a first step toward refinement of the writing skill.
   Through discussion and demonstration the concept of *line* and *space* is developed.
   Lines forming spaces at least 4 to 6 inches high for writing are placed on the blackboard by the teacher. The *meaning of space,* as it appears between the lines (and elsewhere), and the meaning of *line,* and its use on the blackboard and on papers, should be talked over with the children.

   On the top line the teacher* draws "a head." On the second line "a waist" line or "middle." On the third line "two feet." While the children watch, connect the head with the waist, and the waist or middle with the two feet. Explain how some letters begin on the top or head line while others begin on the middle or waist line of the little stick man, and that *all of the letters* follow along the foot or bottom line. Put on the arms and then a long nose to show which direction to go when writing.

   Children should learn to tell and show themselves *before performing,* which line is to be the "foot line" on which the letters will travel, and on which line a particular letter begins. When this "crutch" is no longer needed as a *preventive* measure, it will be discontinued by the children. (Here again, auditory-motor performance precedes the final goal – writing correctly.)
   For a time or two in the beginning, children can be permitted to draw a little stick man on their own papers. However, this is discouraged as soon as the concepts are gained.

*Suggested by Eldra O'Neal and Helen Zylstra, SLD teachers in Renton, Washington.

*Procedure Begins on the Blackboard as an "Input" Learning*

1. The introduction begins on the blackboard where all the children can watch. *Lines to write on* must be used. The teacher directs her own hand as it forms an *h* (or any other letter that has already been taught), speaking in a voice that can be heard easily by *all the children.* She tells them:

   a. Where to start — on the head or top line.

   b. How far down to bring the tall stem — to the foot line.

   c. How far up — and the teacher goes almost to the middle line before rounding to touch the middle or "waist" line, and then going straight down to the foot line.

2. On more *lines made by the teacher,* have individual children go to the blackboard *to make the same letter.* Have the child tell:

   a. Name of letter to be written.

   b. Where the letter begins before writing it, speaking out for all the children to hear and learn.

   c. How far or where the first stroke goes.

   d. How to complete the letter.

Have the child trace over his pattern, naming the letter as it is traced. All the children form the letter in the air, *naming it as it is being formed.*

Wherever necessary, the teacher gives help to reinforce line or arm swing.

Some examples of what children should tell themselves before making a letter are:

With the *p* it begins at the middle line with the stem going below the foot line — then *up over the same line* and around like the *b.* Both *p* and *b* go "out from my body," or, if left-handed, "in front of my body."

With the *a,* it begins a little below the middle line — touches the middle line as it rounds to the foot line — and then all the way up to where it started — and straight down to the foot line — all in one stroke.

*Prevent mistakes* whenever possible. Encourage children to let their heads direct their hands — *to think before doing.*

*Procedure on Lined Paper*

Children are given 12" x 18" newsprint which has been folded in fourths *by the teacher* (at least at this time), with a margin folded at the top on which children write their names.

18"

12"

1.

2.

3.

All children should have their own names which have been written on tagboard by the teacher, the letters at least four to six inches tall for tracing and copying, and for reference whenever needed.

*Auditory-Motor*

To find the foot or writing line, children are asked to put their fingers on the line below the one on which their names were written. It is to be line 1 or the "top line." They move to the next line – line 2 or the "middle line," and then to the next line – line 3 or the "foot or *writing line.*" Some kind of little mark is placed on the writing line to aid in keeping the place, and to show which line letters stand on. (Experienced primary teachers know that this is almost a lesson in itself. Once the children learn how to do this they will acquire this "organizational pattern" which will serve them well in all future work.)

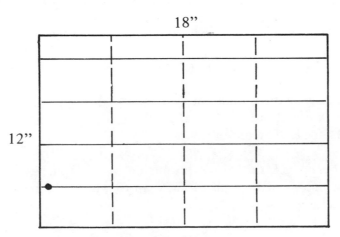

18"

12"

Papers are folded, into fourths, as shown above, enabling each letter to be correctly spaced.

Have a child make a given letter on the blackboard as learned in previous lessons. When finished, the child and the class trace — the child tracing over his pattern, and the children in the air.

The children write the letter on their own papers, always placing their fingers where they will begin — *thinking before doing.* The teacher supervises carefully, giving help and encouragement and approval. Children are encouraged to trace over their own patterns as soon as they are approved.

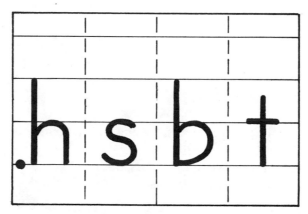

Discourage erasing. Show how to put brackets around misformed "tries" and to make another attempt. Point out that these are "learning papers" and even if mistakes are made, that is how people learn. The "next tries will get better." All this has already been taught in previous lessons and practice, but as most experienced teachers realize, the same kinds of "performance errors" crop up in new kinds of learning situations. Therefore, point out again the importance of *thinking before performing.*

In succeeding lessons have the letters made by the child on the blackboard erased before the class writes on papers — to discourage dependence on copying *in favor of individual effort* to recall.

*Practice to Develop Automatic Recall* (Auditory-Auditory-Visual-Kinesthetic Association)
The children are given folded newsprint.

*The teacher names a letter — one that has been taught during the Learning to Write period.*

1. An individual child *repeats,* forming it in the air, names the *key word,* gives the *sound.*

2. The class repeats, in unison, or some child in need of extra practice is asked to do so.

3. The individual child tells on what line to begin, speaking in a full sentence. (The teacher tells how if the child has difficulty, and *the child then repeats* the teacher's words.)

4. The class writes the letter on its papers, tracing over the letter at least three times.

This is the time to see that the children begin at the left side of the paper and not in the *middle of the page.*

*In Another Lesson*
*The teacher gives the sound of the letter and its key word* by saying:

"Make what says /m/ as in *mother.*"

1. An individual child says: "M — *mother* — /m/."

2. The class repeats.

3. A child tells on what line the letter begins.

4. The class writes the letter on its papers, tracing over its own patterns.

Before the next letter is to be written, discuss the need to keep a "two finger" distance between letters, and show how to measure this distance with fingers.

*Succeeding lessons are given to strengthen the automatic movement from one letter to another.*
After much practice has helped the children acquire reasonable self-reliance and quick recall, it is time to give practice and experience in moving from the writing of one letter to the next with no lapse of time in between. This is something that is necessary when writing words. SLD children need to experience the rhythm in moving from one "unit of performance," such as making a single letter, to the next without long lapses of time in between.

1. *The teacher* names a letter.

2. *An individual child* tells about the letter in the usual way — name — key word — sound.

3. *The class* writes the letter on its papers, traces over its own patterns three or four times, at least.

4. *The teacher* names another letter.

5. *Another child* tells about the letter, and on what line it begins.

6. The class writes the letter and traces. THE CHILDREN ARE REMINDED ABOUT THE "TWO-FINGER" DISTANCE.

Continue with as many letters as space permits.

Discourage erasing in favor of brackets put around the unsatisfactorily made letter and the making of a new letter to serve as a good tracing pattern.

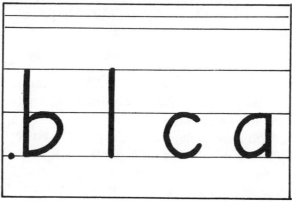

*A more advanced step in succeeding lessons depends on children's previous lessons and practice to gain self-reliance.*

1. The teacher names a letter.

2. The children *tell themselves* its name, key word and sound, write the letter, tracing over their own patterns. If they remember the letter instantly, they write without delay.

3. Then, as the children are tracing, the teacher names another letter without any lapse of time between the completion of tracing one and writing the next.

If children make mistakes, this tells the teacher that previous lessons and practice have gone too fast for the children. If only a few children have difficulty, this indicates which ones need more help, and PINPOINTS THOSE WITH AUDITORY-KINESTHETIC-VISUAL ASSOCIATION difficulties and the need to build their patterns more slowly.

A set of letters for tracing should be left where children can get them to trace in free time. Children whose recall is shown to be weak should be encouraged to practice with these patterns as an independent undertaking. This can be done if children have learned how to trace, copy, and then to write from memory.

The teacher *never ceases to check placement* of letters on correct lines, *spacing* between letters, and *letter formation*, all of which are necessary steps in the preparation for written work.

*Pressure for "speed" is avoided.* The hesitant child is encouraged to look at the *wall cards* as an aid to recall, and *not to guess*.

Sometimes as the teacher is moving about she can say: "Think where to start before beginning," or if there is any hesitation with a letter, such as the 9 "Remember how the letter 9 goes round like an *a* and down below the line and curves under."

These are all structured steps that will enable children to spell words without having to concentrate on *letter formation, placement,* and *distancing* between letters and words. Otherwise, *too much performance is expected, all at one time* of Specific Language Disability children with "dysfunctioning abilities" to handle graphic and sound symbol associations needed for spelling and all written expression.

## B — BLENDING

**Structuring a New Learning** — Blending by Forming Word Entities of Sound and Sight Through the Auditory Approach

So far each letter has been learned as a "single unit" of sight, sound and "feel." The next step is to synthesize learned phonemes — the single units of sound — into purely phonetic words of one syllable that can be *seen*.

From now on, the daily *time block* for teaching will include *blending* in the *Auditory Approach*. A — Alphabet Cards; B — Blending.

---

### LEARNING TO WRITE

Teaching new consonants.
Reviewing consonants already taught in order that they can be carried into the Auditory Approach teaching time for functional use.

---

| AUDITORY APPROACH | VISUAL APPROACH |
|---|---|

 **AUDITORY APPROACH**

A. *Alphabet Cards*

The teacher gives the sound and a child gives the:

1. Name
2. Sound
3. The class repeats (Explained in previous lessons)

Then the teacher exposes the letter for the auditory-visual association. (Refer to pages 53-54.)

Introduce:
B. *Blending* (Encoding) to spell phonetic words

Oral spelling, using the cards in the Chart Holder to make the visual pattern

Writing words on paper

**VISUAL APPROACH**

 A. *Alphabet Cards*

The teacher exposes the card and a child gives the:

1. Names, and forms the letter in the air
2. Names the key word
3. Gives the sound (Refer to page 52-53.)

B. *Unlocking Words* (Decoding) phonetic words

(Not to be attempted at this time. *It follows after blending for Oral Spelling has been taught through the Auditory Approach.*)

| C. *Spelling* | C. *Preparation for Reading* |
|---|---|
| This will become part of the daily teaching time as soon as they learn how to spell orally and to write words on lined paper using correct letter size relationship. | (Refer to pages (175—.) |
| | D. Reading material for which preparation was given under "C" — (Refer to pages 185 and on.) |

Blending begins through the auditory channel of approach which is easier than beginning through a visual approach at this point in children's learning. The visual approach requires visual perception of a "whole" word, whereas in the auditory approach *single units* of sound are put together to make a word. Following the *auditory-perception* of the word, the sequential sounds are associated with the visual symbols, or graphemes, and are arranged with the Alphabet Cards to form the word on the Pocket Chart.

At the same time that children are learning to write letters with correct letter size relationship during the LEARNING TO WRITE period, *blending for oral spelling can begin.* No writing of a word is attempted until the auditory-motor experience of forming words is understood and functional. By first knowing *how* to write and *where* to place letters, and by understanding the need for the sequential arrangement of sounds, the child then can concentrate on the *goal,* which is to write the word that can be spelled. Initial success motivates and encourages individual effort and provides noticeable satisfaction.

*Discussion* precedes the introduction of spelling. In talking together, speak about the way people learned a long time ago that the same sounds in different arrangements made different words. Then letters that stood for the sounds were invented, and by writing them together so they could be seen, people learned to read and to spell and to write. *The children are told that already they have learned so much about letters that they are ready to spell words.*

The Chart Holder is placed before the children. The letters they have learned should be in the pockets.

At the beginning only such purely phonetic words or syllables as can be made *with letters already learned* are used. As soon as the b — h — l — m — t — and the vowel *a* have been learned, the following words and syllables can be blended:

| | | | | | | |
|---|---|---|---|---|---|---|
| lab | tab | bat | tat | lat | hal | mat |
| hat | hab | tal | bab | lal | ham | mam* |

*Blending words* and *learning how to write letters* are taught in two separate periods. Not until a reasonable amount of automatic recall of written letter forms and of how to blend sounds into words (using Alphabet Cards) have been learned are the two combined for written spelling.

*Slingerland, *Teacher's Word Lists.*

*Blending\* — An Auditory-Visual Approach for Oral Spelling*

The first steps serve as an auditory-motor experience for children to feel the sequential placement of each letter in the Pocket Chart to make a word, and this should precede the actual writing of the word.

The introduction of blending may be structured as follows:

1. The teacher pronounces a word — *lab*.

2. All the children repeat — lab — and are asked to *hear* and *feel* the first sound — /l/.

3. An individual child is asked to go to the Chart Holder to give the first sound — /l/, to name the sound — *l* — forming it in the air, and to find its Alphabet Card, which is then placed in a Pocket Chart line, clearly apart from the other letters.

4. Again the word is *repeated by the child* to "feel" how the throat opens. The *vowel sound* is given first, *not its name,* and *then* the child *names* it (saying the key word only if necessary), forming it in the air, and selecting the *a* to place in its proper relationship to the *l*.

5. Again the word is *repeated by the child* so the last sound can be heard and felt, the letter named and associated with its Alphabet Card. The *b* is placed where it belongs to complete the word *lab*. *The word has become a visual as well as a sound pattern.*

6. All the children pronounce the word and write it in the air.

When the children repeat the words named by the teacher it must be remembered that *they see nothing.* They will need to isolate the sequential sounds and to transpose the sounds into graphic symbols, using the Alphabet Cards to build the visual word entities, or patterns.

If a child repeats *lab* and immediately names the vowel because he knows it will be *a,* the teacher says: "Remember you were to give the *sound* of the vowel you heard — not its name. You *cannot see it* until you *hear its sound.* I did not say *labe.* I said *lab.*" *In this way, patterning for hearing vowel sounds, or what "opens the throat," will be built up to serve at a later date when discrimination of vowel sound becomes more important and necessary.*

Children must learn to keep the Alphabet Cards close together, the first consonant card overlapped by the vowel card, and the vowel card overlapped by the next letter, etc., so when grouped, they appear as a "whole" word and not as individual letters strung out over the line. (Refer to page 26.)

7. When use of the word made on the Chart Holder is completed, the cards are replaced in their original alphabetical positions. This can be done by a child.

\*To *blend or encode* phonetic words for independent oral and written spelling, the children learn how to sequence correctly the sound symbols in association with their graphic counterparts.

Another word is given to be worked out in the same way.

> *The object* of this careful patterning is to enable children to think through each sequential step without prompting from the teacher, but until this can be done, the teacher should guide the child's thinking through each step, as given above.

> Sometimes a child forgets the word he is working on, thereby requiring the teacher to give him a clue to its meaning, e.g., if the word is *lab*, tell him it is a place where people experiment or do things with bottles or liquids or try to make something new. If it is a syllable without meaning, such as *hab*, tell the child that it could be part of a bigger word, like *habit — hab it*.

*How The Blending Procedure Can Be Shortened*

As soon as the synthesis of sounds to make words and the need for a vowel sound to "open the throat" are understood, children are able to seek out the vowel sound as soon as the word is pronounced by the teacher.

1. The teacher names the word.

2. The child repeats.

3. The child immediately gives the vowel *sound* that "opens the throat," *not its name.*

4. The child then *names* the vowel, forming it in the air with a free arm swing from the shoulder. The Alphabet Card is placed in a line of the Chart Holder.

5. The child completes the word by placing the consonants in their correct relationship to the vowel, being required to repeat the word whenever a consonant's position needs to be determined. *The child does not guess.*

As new consonants are taught in the LEARNING TO WRITE period, their Alphabet Cards are placed on the Chart Holder. They can be included for *oral spelling.*

*Writing On One-Inch-Space Composition Paper in Preparation for WRITTEN SPELLING and for Reducing the Size of the Letters*

By January, children are usually ready to reduce the size of the letter forms they have learned.

> CAUTION — As new consonants are being taught, do not begin their use in written spelling until they are well learned. They can be used for oral spelling. They are presented by following the initial procedures already given — *tracing* over the Permanent Patterns, *copying* and then *writing from memory*. Letter size relationship is taught, and finally, the letter size is reduced from the folded newsprint to the one inch composition paper.

> As new letters are presented, children begin to learn and to recall gross motor movement patterns in association with sound and visual symbols more quickly.

It is desirable to maintain a standard of performance. What is acceptable to the teacher usually is acceptable to children.

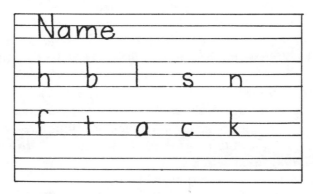

Following the same procedures as given under Practice for Automatic Recall, pages 73-77, dictate learned letters, helping with placement, spacing and the reduced size.

> If a few children with marked kinesthetic-motor weakness find writing is still difficult, let them continue to use lined newsprint with the larger spaces. This is not done as punishment, but is treated with casualness, the teacher commenting that some need more practice than others, and the best time to get it is when people are young. Then continue to help, by guiding children's arms for the rhythm to be felt, and by improving the letter forms with red markers, etc. Encourage the ones with such problems to do well with a fewer number of letters, even if others can accomplish more. Momentum is gathered when success is met with only a few, rather than failure with many.

> The patient, persisting, specific language disability teacher who does not "give up" over a child's prolonged difficulties, brings about wonderful response in achievement and self-confidence. A teacher needs to be self-reminded that

individuals do not work at the same levels or at the same tempo or with the same capacities, abilities and disabilities. Often required is over-teaching with honest evaluation without undue praise for something a child recognizes as unjustified. He is not discouraged when told: "It isn't as good as it is going to be when you have had more time to work at it. Keep right on trying and you will see how much better you do."

*Blending — An Auditory-Visual-Kinesthetic Approach to Written Spelling*

After the patterning for oral spelling, and the ability to recall and to write letters have been well established, different children are chosen to work out teacher-named phonetic words with the Alphabet Cards on the Chart Holder *and then to write them.*

1. A child works out a given word on the Chart Holder.

2. The same child leaves the word in the Chart Holder where the class, but not the child, can see it. He goes to the blackboard, *names,* and then *writes* the·word in the air for the teacher to see that the recall is going to be right.

3. Last, the child writes the word *on lines made by the teacher* on the blackboard. The class observes, checking with the word that was left on the Chart Holder.

If recall is lost before the word can be written, have the child work out the word again, this time writing the letters on the blackboard as each letter is named.

Have the letters kept close together in order that the completed word looks like a word.

When a word has been successfully written, all the children *pronounce* it first and then *write* it in the air, *naming* each letter as it is formed. At the same time, the child at the blackboard traces over his pattern on the blackboard.

Different children are given turns to go through the same procedure with phonetic words. Choose children who will probably meet with success for the first turns, and then the weaker ones for their turns. This affords the weaker ones more time to grasp the procedure, but be sure not to neglect giving them their turns because self-confidence will not be built without this Auditory-Visual-Kinesthetic and Motor experience under the teacher's understanding guidance.

*Using the Lined One-Inch-Spaced Composition Paper*

Each child is given a sheet of one-inch-spaced composition paper.
Following lessons previously described:

1. Have a child work out a word on the Chart Holder in the usual way for all to see and hear.

2. The same child then writes the word on the blackboard.

3. All the children pronounce the word when it is completed, write it in the air as the child at the board traces over his own word pattern.

4. Then the word on the blackboard *is erased* and the one on the Chart Holder *is covered*. When this is done, all the children write on their papers.

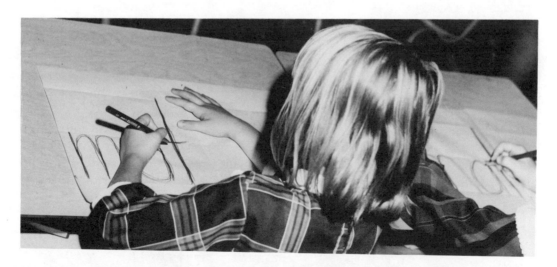

The teacher circulates to watch performance, *preventing* mistakes whenever possible. This is a "learning lesson," where teachers give immediate help and guidance.

Correcting papers at a later time, unless the teacher works directly with the child, is of little benefit. Better for the child is immediate help to insure *correct impressions* will be perceived for integration and storage if recall and performance patterns are to be reliable.

5. When finished, the word on the Chart Holder is uncovered for checking and matching.

Another word is worked out in the same way.

*Shortening the Above Procedure*

As soon as children gain self-confidence and can write words successfully, it is advisable to have the given word worked out on the Chart Holder, then covered to help children learn to depend upon themselves, and written by the children. When all are finished, the word on the Chart is exposed.

In time, the teacher can: 1) Name a word, 2) a child works it out orally, 3) all the children repeat the word and spell and write it in the air, 4) all the children write the word on their papers.

These last procedures should not be hurried. Secure thought and performance patterns are more important. When children are *ready,* the shortened steps come about naturally.

*Teaching Children How to Organize*

The written spelling lessons provide good opportunity for guidance in organizing work done on paper. The lack of this ability is often a handicap to children in the years ahead. For ordered arrangement on their papers:

1. Children's names should be written on the top spaces before the written spelling of words.

2. Placement of words, beginning at the left side of the paper should be emphasized.

3. Consistent placement of words, either written one *under* the other, or one *after* the other, with two-finger spacing, prevents words from being written all over the pages.

   For the child who learns to organize his work (auditory-motor), concentration then can be focused on the "thought pattern" used to spell words. It need not be confused by inexperience in writing within smaller spaces or by trying to recall letter size, placement, and form.

UNTIL BLENDING OF PHONEMES INTO "WORD UNITS" THROUGH THE AUDITORY APPROACH IS FULLY COMPREHENDED AND FUNCTIONAL, NO ATTEMPT TO INTRODUCE UNLOCKING OF WORDS THROUGH THE VISUAL APPROACH IS UNDERTAKEN.

EXAMPLES OF HOW TO PLAN DAILY LESSONS FOR LEARNING TO WRITE AND THE AUDITORY APPROACH PERIODS:

**Example 1 of a Daily Lesson Plan**

LEARNING TO WRITE

| | |
|---|---|
| *Teach f.* | Place Wall Card for all to see (Refer to pages 40 and 52.) |
| | Trace over Permanent Pattern |
| | Copy |
| | Write from memory |

Review:      b  c  s  t  l  h        using 1" lined paper

| | |
|---|---|
| Teacher: | Names a letter, e.g., *c.* |
| Child: | Repeats letter name, forming in the air, names key word, gives sound. |
| Class: | Repeats. |
| Child: | Tells where to begin: "A little below the middle line." |
| Class: | Writes the letter on paper. Traces over own patterns until teacher names next letter (Refer to pages 73, 74.) |

Follow the same procedure with each letter.

The teacher must be sure to circulate about the classroom to make sure correct letter forms are being made. Using red markers, strengthen or correct a line for an individual child's particular tracing need.

AUDITORY APPROACH

A.   *Alphabet Cards*

Place the Chart Holder where all can see.

| | |
|---|---|
| Teacher: | Give the sound of one of the already learned letters. |
| Child: | Names letter, forming in the air, names the key word, gives sound. Finds the matching letter card and holds it up for all to see, (an A-V Association). |
| Class: | Together the children tell about the letter, (a V-A-K Association). |

Follow the same procedure with sounds of other letters.

B. *Blending*
   Use 1" composition paper (or folded newsprint — page 72.)
   Use words or syllables made with already taught letters, e.g.,

   sal  tab  cast  and some made with the newly taught
   letter *f*  — fat  taf  fast  fam

   Teacher:    Names a word.
   Child:      Repeats word.
               Builds word with cards, (Refer to page 82).
               Writes word on blackboard.
               Work is then covered.
   Class:      Writes word on paper (page 83).

C. *Spelling*

Have the children trace over their name cards (made by the teacher early in the year) with wrong end of pencil or with two fingers, then copy, and, finally, without looking. Be sure to have children name the letters softly, but distinctly, as they are formed and traced.

**Example 2 of Daily Lesson Plan**

LEARNING TO WRITE

Use folded newsprint, as shown below:

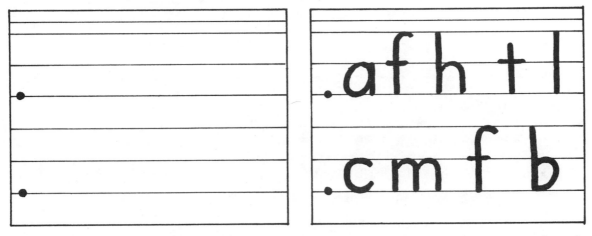

Review letters already taught with emphasis on the most recently learned letter, i. e., *f*, if it was the last one.

| | |
|---|---|
| Teacher: | Dictate a letter. |
| Class: | Repeat, forming in air. Write on paper, tracing over its own patterns, *naming* the letter with each tracing, and continuing until the next letter is named. |
| Teacher: | After children have had time for from 4 - 6 tracings, name the next letter without allowing any break between the writing of one letter and the need to move on to the next one  (page 75). |

The child (or children), who is very weak in the Kinesthetic-motor area, should not be pressed to work beyond his ability. Allow him to continue practicing one letter for as long as needed, even if others can move faster. Then when he finishes, allow him to continue with the next one dictated to the others. It is better for such a child to do well with a few than to try to keep up and fail with most.

## AUDITORY APPROACH

A.   *Alphabet Cards*

f   l   c   a   m   b   h   s   k   ck (if taught)

| | |
|---|---|
| Teacher: | Gives the *sound* and *key word*. (When the children are sure of sound-symbol association, the key word may be left out. However, this should not be done until children are sure of association without the help of the key word.) |
| Child: | *Names letter,* forming in air, *names key word* and *gives the sound.* |
| Teacher: | Shows the card *after* the child has told the name and sound. This is done to reinforce the auditory-visual association. |

Continue in the same way for each letter.

When the teacher asks: "What says /k/ as in cake?" the child must name *c*; if /k/ as in kite?" it must be *k*; and if /k/ as in Jack?, it must be *ck*.

If the teacher asks: "What says /k/?" and gives no key word, the *child* must answer by telling all three ways of spelling the sound /k/—or any one of the three ways.

> k - kite - /k/
> c - cake - /k/
> ck - Jack - /k/

This is an initial learning for eventual dictionary use.

B.  *Blending*

Use the Chart Holder
1" spaced composition paper.
Words or syllables: tam   fab   sat   cab   hal   faf

| | |
|---|---|
| Teacher: | Pronounces a word, e.g., *tam.* |
| Child: | Repeats. Gives the vowel *sound.* |
| | Places the vowel card on a line of the Chart Holder. Repeats the word. Names and places the first consonant, *t* on the line. Places the *a* in such a way that it overlaps the *t* card, naming it as he does so, and adds the last letter *m.* Whenever the sequence of sound is lost, have the child repeat the word. (Errors in retention and recall can be detected by the teacher and often by the child, himself.) |
| Class: | Pronounces and writes word in the air. |
| Teacher: | Covers the word. |
| Class: | Writes the word on paper. (Refer to pages 82, 83.) |

Before the next word is worked out and written, children should be reminded about how words are to be written, one under the other, or across the line with a two-finger space between words. They should be given experience using both organizations (page 84).

THESE ARE NOT MEANT TO BE THE ONLY WAYS PRACTICE AND TEACHING ARE GIVEN—JUST TWO DAILY PLANS. A creative teacher will approach each day's lesson in a little different way. Only the basic principles involved should not be changed.

INTRODUCING A NEW VOWEL — Short i

Usually by January children are ready to learn another vowel. Short *i* is introduced.

LEARNING TO WRITE

1. The Wall Card is held before the children, both its *name* and *key word* given and its *sound.*

   Teacher: "This letter is *i.* It is another vowel whose sound opens our throats to help us get from one sound to another in the same way the vowel *a* does. Its key word is *Indian* and we can hear its *sound* right at the beginning of the word *Indian* — like this: /ĭ/ — Indian."

   "We tell about the vowel *i* by saying: '*I — Indian — /ĭ/,*' to help us remember."

   Give the children turns to tell about the vowel *i* as they look at the Wall Card, each child saying: "*I — Indian — /ĭ/.*"

2. Give each child a *Permanent Pattern* for tracing (pages 45-46) with the first two fingers, or the wrong end of the pencil. By this time they should be familiar with the practice procedure to feel the gross motor movement. They should name the letter as it is written.

   If preferred, let them trace over teacher-made patterns on the blackboard instead of using the Permanent Patterns. Point out letter-size relationship and on what line the *i* begins.

3. Because the *i* is easy to make, children can be given the expendable patterns made by the teacher to trace (page 47), copy in the second space, and then to fold the first section of the paper over the second section (page 48) in readiness for writing from memory in the third space.

   The Wall Card is pinned on the wall.

   The two *i* Alphabet Cards are placed on the Chart Holder on the same line with, and following, the vowel *a* cards.

| AUDITORY APPROACH | VISUAL APPROACH |
|---|---|
| A. *Alphabet Cards* | A. *Alphabet Cards* |
| Include the *i* in the practice of drill where the *sound* is given by the teacher, and a child making the association of the *sound* with the *visual symbol* says: "I - Indian - /ĭ/," remembering to form the letter in the air as it is named to include the kinesthetic-motor association. | As soon as *i* has been learned, it should be included in the visual drill where cards are *exposed* for children, individually, to *name, name the key word* and make the association by giving the sound. |
| Here the initial stimulus comes through the ears. | Here the initial stimulus comes through the eyes. |
| B. *Blending* (encoding) | B. *Unlocking* (decoding) |
| | (Refer to green pages.) |

Use only words made with consonants already learned and the vowel *i*.

Do not confuse the children by requiring discrimination of vowel sound until *how to discriminate* is taught in succeeding lessons.

1. *For auditory perception* of the short vowel *i* sound, name a different word containing short *i* for each child.

> Child: Repeats the word. Feels how throat opens and listens for the vowel sound.
> Gives short *i* sound.
> Names the *i*, forming it in the air.

NO ATTEMPT TO SPELL THE WORD IS REQUIRED.

Examples of words that can be used are:

| | | | | |
|---|---|---|---|---|
| lip | hid | sniff | wrist | itch |
| clip | shrimp | drift | snip | crib |

If the child has difficulty perceiving, over-emphasize the vowel sound; e.g., if the word is *snip,* say *sni* (prolonging the /ĭ/). Let the child try again.

Sometimes over-emphasize the sound by allowing the child to see how the teacher's throat opens.

With others it helps by speaking and over-emphasizing at the side of the child's head, but *not* into his ear or face.

2. *Using the Chart Holder and Alphabet Cards,* have individual children make words (pages 78-81) or syllables named by the teacher. For example, if the consonants that have already been learned h l k f c g m s t b w and the consonant digraph ck, such words as the following could be used.

| wig | lit | lift | him | wit | fig | wilt |
|-----|-----|------|-----|-----|-----|------|
| tick (tic tik) bib | | wick | *will* (tell children there are two l's) | | | |

3. *Writing short i words* (pages 82-85) as an advancing step in working out words containing short i, should follow blending a word on the Chart Holder. Cover the word and have the children write on lined composition paper or on folded newsprint.

4. A step in advance of the above is to have a child work out a word orally by: a. *Repeating* the word *named by the teacher and not by a child, who may make an incorrect selection.* b. Giving the vowel sound, c. Naming the vowel, forming it in the air, and d. Spelling orally, forming the letters in the air.

The class pronounces the same word and spells orally while forming the letters.

All the children write on their papers (following the directions for word placement organization given on page 84.)

Continue in the same way with other short i words for as many lessons as it takes until its use is reasonably functional.

It should be remembered that some children will be able to do all the words a teacher dictates while others cannot. It is better for such children to do fewer in number, and do them right, than to fail in trying to "keep pace" with those who can write and perform more rapidly. In time their momentum increases.

STRUCTURING A NEW LEARNING — Vowel Discrimination of short *a* and short *i*

Here is where children begin to learn to listen for the difference in vowel sound, which is one of the necessary keys to successful spelling of purely phonetic and, eventually, ambiguously spelled words.

The Green Flag (go ahead) words refer to those spelled exactly as they sound, such as: *bat - sam - him - tilt.*

The Yellow Flag (caution) words refer to those whose *sounds* can be spelled in more than one way, such as *creme* or *creem* for *cream,* or *cote* for *coat.* They require thought for meaning and memory to be gained through "over practice." This is an initial step leading to future use of dictionary skills and is presented in the second year continuum.

The Red Flag (stop and remember) words refer to those of irregular spelling that must be "over-learned" and remembered such as *was - want - laugh.* (Refer to page 121.)

## AUDITORY APPROACH

B.  *Blending*

Tell the children they will need to listen carefully because the words to be named will have either the /ă/ or /ĭ/ (which they have been learning) sound. They need not think about *how* to spell the word, but only the vowel sound that opens their throats and its name. Remind them that this is the hard part of spelling any word, and when they are able to do this, it will not be difficult to spell the word.

*Auditory Perception and Discrimination of Short Vowels a and i*

1. The teacher names a different word or syllable containing either short i or short i for each child to have a turn to:

   a. Repeat the word
   b. Give the vowel *sound*
   c. Name the vowel, forming it in the air.

   *No spelling* should be attempted since this is *for perception alone.* Words that are too difficult for them to spell *can and should be used,* such as:

| | | | | | |
|---|---|---|---|---|---|
| lad | lip | crisp | rant | spin | bliss |
| limp | lamp | blast | witch | smash | cast* |

*Slingerland, *Teacher's Word Lists.*

2. *To vary the listening game* and to strengthen the auditory-visual association, sometimes have each child go through the above procedure and then select the correct vowel card from the Chart Holder for all the class to see.

3. In still another lesson, let each child write the correct vowel on the blackboard after following the first procedure.

After children are able to perceive and discriminate vowel sounds, they are ready to spell the words named by the teacher.

A child having more auditory confusion than most should be given extra help. The teacher should *over-emphasize the vowel sound,* and always have the child repeat the word to *hear and feel* the vowel sound. *Encourage the child to make instant selection of the vowel Alphabet Card, since visual perception and recall in association with the A-K may be more dependable and easier "to hold" than an initial stimulus carried over the auditory sensory channel. But such a child should be helped with auditory perception and given teacher-controlled practice to strengthen this association to the fullest possibility.*

*Vowel Discrimination in Blending Words and Syllables Using Alphabet Cards on the Chart Holder* (Refer to Visual Approach, page 166.)

1. A child is given a turn at the Chart Holder while the class watches.

The teacher names either a short *i* or a short *a* word.

The child:
   a. Repeats the word
   b. Gives the vowel sound
      (The teacher needs to remember that the word is *not seen,* so that *the initial stimulus will go through the child's ear as an auditory sound.*)
   c. Names and forms the vowel
   d. Places the vowel card on a line clearly apart from the other cards
   e. Repeats the word and places all the Alphabet Cards in correct relationship to each other

   (Be sure the child names the first letter, or letters, as they are placed, names and overlaps the vowel card (page 26), and any consonant that follows, making certain that the letters are named and *felt* in correct sequence.)

   All this requires Auditory-Visual-Kinesthetic association with a body or motor response in the sequential placement of the cards by the arm and *should precede the actual writing of the word.*

Other children are given turns.

2. Following the same procedure, as given above, have the child write the word from memory on the blackboard, *on teacher-made lines,* while the class watches. The children, but not the child at the blackboard, can see the Chart Holder and know if the word is being written correctly.

When a child gets to the blackboard, if he forgets how he made the word on the Chart Holder, have him repeat the word and then write each letter as he gives each succeeding sound and name.

The class names and writes the word in the air. Give turns to other children.

Do not overlook the child who may be having considerable difficulty. Give more help by guiding him through each successive step to make certain he experiences successful completion of the word. *This is not the time to call upon another child to "show him how to do it." It is the place for teacher guidance.*

*Vowel Discrimination — Writing Words on Folded Newsprint or 1" Composition Paper*

1. In another lesson, follow the same procedure. After the word is written on the blackboard for all to see, have it erased and the word on the Chart Holder covered.

All the children write the word on their papers, being sure to write them across the paper or, one below the other, whichever way the teacher directs.

The teacher circulates around the room, preventing mistakes and helping where needed.

Continue with other words in the same way.

2. As soon as vowel discrimination in oral and written spelling of phonetic short *a* and short *i* words becomes reasonably functional, the teacher can name a word and have an individual child:

    a. Repeat the word
    b. Give vowel sound, then its name, repeat the word and spell orally, writing in the air.

The children repeat and write in the air first and then write on their papers, eliminating use of the Chart Holder and blackboard.

The teacher moves about *preventing* mistakes, sometimes reforming with a red pencil a poorly made letter for a child to trace. Others may benefit from reassurance, encouragement or commendation.

*Test infrequently* (except to discover teacher need for emphasis), but give children much practice. *Over-teach.*

3. On another day have large composition paper folded in half. The children write their names in the top spaces in correct letter-size relationship. At the head of each column, have them write a and i as shown below:

```
 _____
|  Name         |           |
|_____|_____|
|_____|_____|
|       a       |     i     |
|_____|_____|
|_____|_____|
|_____|_____|
|_____|_____|
|_____|_____|
|_____|_____|
|_____|_____|
|_____|_____|
```

Follow the same procedures already given, but after a child spells his word orally, followed by the class writing in the air, have him tell in which column it should be written. All the children write accordingly.

Words are not placed for children to copy because they should learn early to depend upon themselves and to gain self-confidence.

Again, the teacher moves about, preventing mistakes, guiding, encouraging and approving.

Papers can be saved and used in another lesson if there is ample space left.

*Substituting a Consonant or a Vowel Within a Word*

Use the Chart Holder.
In the usual way, have a child make a word such as *cap.*
The teacher can say: "If that word is *cap,* what part must change to make *cap* say *tap*?"
The child may say: "The first letter," or 'The *c.*"

*Do not accept the act of pointing* to the *c* as sufficient. Have the child *verbalize* the act, even if the teacher must say the correct words for the child to repeat. This is an area in which far too many children collapse—inability to verbalize a performance, or a plan, or an accomplishment.

Have the child make the substitution, returning the c to its original place on the Chart Holder.

The teacher can say: "Yes, you put the *t* in place of the *c* which makes the word say *tap*."

Continue in the same way, changing *tap* to *tab* and then *tab* to *tib*.

Each time have the child *feel the body movement* of putting one letter in place of another and then *verbalizing his performance*. Each time the teacher can follow the child's performance by saying: "Yes, you substituted the __ for __."

Before long, a discussion of the word *substitute* will become meaningful, and the concept applied to "a substitute teacher" as one who takes the place of another may help clarify the meaning of the word.

*More Examples of How to Plan Daily Lessons for Learning to Write and for the Auditory Approach Periods are shown on the following pages.*

**Example 3 of a Daily Lesson Plan**

LEARNING TO WRITE

*Review and Practice*

1. Each child is given folded newsprint or 1 inch space composition paper.

Dictate letters learned (refer to page 73-74) for practice in automatic recall. Assuming the following have been taught, use l h a t i b s m c g f k ck).

AUDITORY APPROACH

A. *Alphabet Cards*

Holding the Alphabet Cards that have been taught *but not exposing them,* the teacher gives the sound of one.

A child:

1. Names the letter, forming it in the air
2. Names the key word
3. Gives the sound.

*The teacher* exposes the card for all to see for the auditory-visual association.

Continue giving all children turns, letting the class repeat after each child's performance.

B. *Blending*

Follow the same procedure as given on pages 94, 95, and 96, using the following words:

|     |     |     |      |
|-----|-----|-----|------|
| bit | him | mit |      |
| sill (tell children to put two l's) | | | |
| lick (tell children that *ck* is the way to spell the /k/ sound) | | | |
| sick | | | |
| ham | hat | hit | hill |

The teacher's plans may include more words than there is time to write, but more than enough material always should be planned. Children enjoy writing when they know how and seldom want to stop.

**Example 4 of a Daily Lesson Plan**

LEARNING TO WRITE

Introduce, for example, the consonant p. (Refer to pages 42-49 and to page 52.)

Each child traces over the Permanent Pattern and then with a pencil on an expendable pattern as shown on page 46.

The Wall Card is placed on the wall and the two Alphabet Cards on the Chart Holder. From now on the consonant *p* can be included in blending words on the Chart Holder. *Until the letter-size relationship is taught, the* p *should not be used in writing words* - to insure correct writing from the beginning.

AUDITORY APPROACH

A.  *Alphabet Cards*
    l  h  a  t  i  b  s  m  c  g  f  h  ck  p

The teacher puts lines on the blackboard on which the children will write letters, one child at a time.

———————————————————————————————————

———————————————————————————————————

———————————————————————————————————

A child is chosen to go to the blackboard and *the teacher* asks: "What says /k/ as in kite?"

The child (facing the blackboard so the class will not see the letter formed backwards in the air, as it would be if he faced the class), answers by saying "*k* (forming in the air) *kite* /k/."

Then the child writes the letter on the blackboard, naming it as it is written.

While he traces over his pattern two or three times, the rest of the class writes in the air.

Continue in the same way, giving turns to different children. Help children to leave sufficient spacing between each letter since these are single letters and not being used to make words at this time.

B.  *Blending on the Chart Holder*

Give individual children turns to work out words, using the Alphabet Cards, such as:

| tap | pam | cap | lip | big |
|------|------|------|------|------|
| bib | hilt | gas | gasp | pick |
| last | past | list | lisp | |

Whenever a letter is newly introduced, such as the *p,* use it in many word arrangements before expecting children to write it.

**Example 5 of a Daily Lesson**

LEARNING TO WRITE

Teach the letter-size relationship of the consonant *p*.

1. Make several patterns on the blackboard for different children to trace, as shown below.

   The teacher points out on which line to begin, *telling* the children what she is doing while she forms the letter, by saying: "The stem begins on the middle line—above the foot or writing line—and goes down below the writing line, then up and, just like the *b*, it goes out from (or across) my body. It is all made with one stroke." (Refer to pages 62 and 63.)

   Give several children at a time turns to trace over the teacher-made patterns. Make fresh patterns for other children who are called upon to have turns.

2. Next, each child is given folded newsprint on which a dot is placed on the "writing line." (Refer to page 72.)

   Again speak about where the *p* will begin, have all children place fingers on the line where the letter starts and then write the *p*.

   The teacher should make patterns for any child who may have difficulty, and in all cases, check each child's pattern before giving the "go ahead and trace" signal. With a red pencil, improve any line for a child to make sure the tracing pattern is a good one.

   When children are ready, they copy, and when sure, turn papers over, dot the writing line, and write from memory.

   The children's standards will depend greatly on those of the teacher.

AUDITORY APPROACH

A.   *Alphabet Cards*

Follow same directions as given on page 98.

B.    *Blending*

Practice using the cards on Chart Holder *and lines made on the blackboard by the teacher.*
Give individual children turns to work out words on the Chart Holder (pages 93-94-95 and then to write the word on the blackboard while the class watches.
Then the class repeats the word and writes it in the air.
Examples of words that can be given are:

|      |      |      |      |      |
|------|------|------|------|------|
| lamp | past | map  | lag  | gas  |
| gap  | pit  | sip  | sap  | tip  |

If a child writes *lap* for *lamp,* the teacher tells him his word says *lap.* He may recognize his omission. Otherwise, over-emphasize the omitted sound to help the child hear for himself and make his own correction.

**Example 6 of a Daily Lesson**

Combining LEARNING TO WRITE (a review of letters already taught) and
A.   *The Alphabet Cards*—an Auditory-Visual and Kinesthetic-Motor experience.

The children are given 1" space composition paper on which they write their names.
Have the papers folded to make four columns enabling one letter to be written under another in each of the four columns.

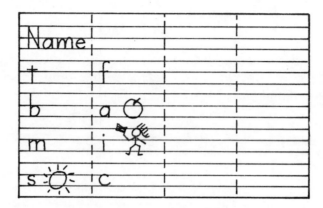

A child is asked to tell, e.g., what says /t/ as in *turtle?*
The child does so in the usual way, the class repeats and each child writes the letter on the paper.

While the teacher is helping one of the reading groups during the Visual Approach period, the other children can draw key word pictures after each of the letters written on the paper as shown above.

B.   *Blending*

Practice on the Chart Holder.
Give turns to individual children to work out phonetic words* that require double consonant beginnings or endings, such as:   ·

| | | | | |
|---|---|---|---|---|
| raft | clap | slam | slim | sift |
| cliff (tell the child to use two f's) | | | | |
| mist | mast | skim | (encourage children to ask if | |

(encourage children to ask if
*c* or *k* should be used, telling
them which is right. They should
be taught that *ck* never is used
at the beginning of a word or
syllable.)

*Slingerland, *Teacher's Word Lists.*

## C — SPELLING

### Planning Ahead

Continue to teach and to bring into functional use more of the consonants.

Usually by February the short vowel *u* is introduced. It requires no new kind of learning because by now children understand the use of vowels, and they should have acquired the "thought pattern" for both listening for and discriminating vowel sounds.

Teacher judgment must determine readiness for the introduction of the short vowel *o* — probably in March.

For some children, or even the entire class, short *e* should be postponed until late spring, or possibly until the Second Year Continuum. The discrimination of short *i* and short *e* should not be undertaken until the *i* is well learned. The *e* can be in evidence on the *Vowel Chart,* however, for the benefit of those who already can "abstract" and use it functionally as a result of previous experience with the other vowels. Its *letter form* should be taught without its sound when needed for writing the suffix *ed,* etc., (page 133) if not before.

After both letters which make a consonant digraph when combined have been learned, a consonant digraph, such as *sh,* can be introduced. The *sh* Alphabet Card should be included in the Teacher Alphabet Pack for drill and with others on the Chart Holder for functional use in blending.

Suggested word list:

| | | | | | |
|---|---|---|---|---|---|
| ship | sham | shift | shaft | shuck | hash |
| fish | wish | bash | lash | dish | cash |
| shut | shack | dash | sash | | |

The same plan should be followed with other digraphs — *ck* — *ch* — *wh* — *th\**. Do not teach *ch* until *ck* is well learned because they look so much alike that they might be confused.

The Daily Organization to guide a teacher's planning for the second half of the first year is shown on the next page. All that has been learned leads into functional use for spelling.

*\*Ibid.

**Daily Organization of Instruction**

---

### LEARNING TO WRITE

#### Teaching New Consonants

Review consonants already taught so they can be carried into the *Auditory Approach teaching time* for functional use in writing and into the *Visual Approach* for auditory-visual association.

Teach how to write consonant digraphs – *ck* – sh – ch – th – wh *and suffixes* – ing – ed – er – es, *whenever they are introduced for functional use.*

---

| AUDITORY APPROACH | VISUAL APPROACH |
|---|---|
| **(A.)** *Alphabet Cards* | **(A.)** *Alphabet Cards* |
| Each day's lesson should begin with at least 4-10 minutes of practice. (Refer to pages 53-54.) | Each day's work should begin with a few minutes of practice or drill. (Refer to pages 52, 154 and 155.) |
| **(B.)** *Blending Phonetic Words* | **(B.)** *Unlocking Phonetic Words* |
| Oral spelling, using the cards on Chart Holder for auditory-visual association OR Writing on paper, following oral spelling. (Refer to Page 77-98.) | (Refer to green pages – page 157–.) |
| **(C.)** *Spelling* | **(C.)** *Preparation for Reading* |
| 1. Green flag – phonetic words. | (Refer to green pages – page 174–) |
| 2. Red flag – "words to be learned" or irregularly spelled words. | The four Steps with Words and Phrases (Refer to page 175.) |
| 3. Yellow flag – ambiguous spelling comes in Second Year Continuum. | |

—Adding suffixes
—Writing phrases
—Writing sentences
(Refer to bottom of
pages 116 and 126.)

D.  *Dictation*

Used in Second Year Continuum

(E.)  *Independent & Creative Writing*

(Refer to page 144.)

(D.)  *Reading*

(Refer to green pages — page 185—.)

(E.)  *Independent Reading*

**Using the Daily Organization for Lesson Planning**

TO THE TEACHER

A foresighted teacher of SLD children will plan daily lessons to follow successive structured steps that provide practice and constant review adapted to the children's rate and "tempo" of learning, and their security in functional use of whatever has been taught. Therefore, it would be contrary to the purpose of this Guide to "program" day-to-day lessons for the teacher to follow. The children themselves and the teacher's familiarity and experience with the successive steps must determine daily planning.

The Daily Format and the examples of daily lessons included herein serve as guides for both approaches, one devoted to the Auditory Approach and the other to the Visual Approach. The third period, usually preceding the Auditory Approach, should be planned for Learning to Write, in which new letter forms are taught, and practice and review are provided for automatic recall and smooth rhythm in moving from one letter to the next.

Experience and adherence to the instructional technique brings security and skill to the teacher which is then reflected in children's success and attitudes.*

SOME "POINTERS" FOR TEACHERS TO FOLLOW IN USING THE DAILY ORGANIZATION TO GUIDE THEIR DAILY LESSON PLANNING

LEARNING TO WRITE

*This is not a period in which to teach how to spell.* It is for *writing* so children can acquire automatic recall of each letter's *name, feel,* and *sound* for functional use in written work and for automatic recognition in reading.

AUDITORY APPROACH

A.  *Alphabet Cards*

The teacher gives the *sound* of the letter, consonant digraph or suffix.

The child:

1. *Names* the letter (or letters), forming it with his arm
2. *Names* the key word
3. Gives the *sound* of the letter, digraph or suffix.

When using the *suffix cards,* the teacher says: "What suffix says *ing?*" *and the child answers: "i-n-g," but does not give a key word.*

---

*Years of observation and reports from many teachers have shown that it takes at least two years, usually under some guidance, to acquire skill with the technique.

106

With the suffix *ed,* the teacher need only to ask what letters make the "past time" suffix because, at this point, the three sounds of the suffix *ed* have not been taught. (Refer to page 133.)

4. The teacher exposes the card for the auditory-visual association, and the class repeats.

B.   *Blending* (Encoding)

Each day's lesson should provide practice in sounding out purely phonetic, short vowel, one-syllable words for Auditory-Visual association. When the word is pronounced, or written, a Kinesthetic association is added.

On some days, just the Chart Holder need be used.

On other days, the words should be written on lined paper after they are spelled orally—to prevent unnecessary mistakes.

Practice in using any newly introduced vowel is given within this time block.

C.   *Spelling*

As soon as children have learned how to recognize and to write letters, and to blend and discriminate at least two vowel sounds, they are ready for both oral and written spelling of one syllable, short vowel, purely phonetic words (Green Flag). **This carries on to use of suffixes, to writing phrases and to writing sentences.**

How to learn Red Flag words begins when they are needed for phrase writing. (Refer to page 121.)

All this experience leads to independent or creative writing, and it prepares readiness for dictation at a later date.

D.   *Dictation*

How to study for, and to write several sentences to make a paragraph is introduced and explained in the Second Year Continuum.

E.   *Independent and Creative Writing*

Spontaneous attempts at written self-expression begin—usually in early spring—as an outgrowth of children's discovery of their newly acquired power to verbalize, to spell, and to write, and even how to study what they wish to learn to use.

Suggestions to assist those who may hesitate, or are too cautious to try, are given on page 144. Opportunity can be provided for those with more independence and readiness enabling them to progress more rapidly than the majority.

**Structuring a New Learning — Use of Suffixes — *ing,* with Concept**

As soon as children can use the short vowels *a* and *i* to spell one-syllable, phonetic words, they are ready to begin learning how to use suffixes. From the start, this is undertaken "through the intellect."

The introduction and structuring of *suffix concept and functional use* are taught in the *Auditory Approach,* C.—Spelling.

Begin with the suffix *ing.*

*First Step* — Concept — Verbalizing

The teacher says to the children:

"When we lift something, the word *lift* tells what we *do.* Using that same word — *lift* — how do we make the word *lift* tell what we are doing?"

> If a child starts to give the *meaning* of *lift,* point out that the meaning was not asked for and while it is fine that it is understood, what is wanted is how the word *lift* can be made to tell what we are *doing.*

> Some child will say the right word — *lifting.*

"Yes, *lifting* tells what we are *doing.* What do you hear at the end of the word *lift* that makes it say lift*ing*?"

Some of the children will hear and tell — /*ing*/.

The teacher writes *ing* in manuscript on the blackboard, and holds up an Alphabet Card on which *ing* appears, and tells the children that *ing* is an "ending" to a word and is called a suffix. It is added to many words that tell what we *do* to make them tell what we are *doing.*

> *Ing* is learned as a "whole" — an auditory-visual-kinesthetic association related to concept.

Children are told that /*ing*/ does not have any meaning by itself, but when added to some words that do have meaning, those words have their meaning changed a little.

The teacher says:

"Let us see how that works. *Camp* tells what we do. What are we *doing* when we camp?"

A child will say "camping," and the teacher should point to *ing,* either on the blackboard or on the Chart Holder to assist children in visual-auditory association.

Use many words — with no thought of how they are spelled — such as:

| | | | | |
|---|---|---|---|---|
| jump | scream | hop | play | push |
| trim | look | hope | point | cook |
| cry | laugh | wish | love | pout |
| shout | hug | walk | hunt | stretch |

Here is an opportunity to play games, one such game being to let a child *tell what he can do* and then perform to *show how he is doing it.*

*Second Step* — Oral Spelling, with Visual Association as the Words are Made with Cards on the Chart Holder
Teach under B - Blending in Daily Organization

With beginners, no word that requires doubling the final consonant, no silent e word, and no non-phonetic word should be used. The teacher structures each successive step in children's learning to help them acquire the desired "thought pattern," which is: *Root word,* plus *suffix,* with the change it makes in expressing action, and the understanding and concept of the purpose of suffixes.

From now on an Alphabet Card *"ing"* should be kept on the Chart Holder and in the teacher's Alphabet Card pack.
A child is asked to work out a word pronounced by the teacher, such as *"limp."* The child should always follow the usual procedure in technique as given on page 80.
When completed, the child is asked to *tell* what must be done to make the word *limp* tell what he is *doing* when he limps. Help the child to verbalize in order for him to say, "I will add *ing,*" or "I will add the suffix *ing.*"
The child places the *ing* card in its correct relationship to the root word. He steps back for all to see. He and the class spell the word orally as they form the letters with arm swings.
Cards should be replaced in their correct places on the Chart Holder before another child is given a turn with a word selected by the teacher from a suggested word list such as:

| | | | | | |
|---|---|---|---|---|---|
| camp | dash | limp | lift | wish | list |
| stamp | tramp | mash | mask | fish | ask |

*Third Step* — Written Spelling — Auditory-Visual-Kinesthetic Association

Each child needs his own sheet of 1" composition paper.

1. An individual child is asked to form a word, dictated by the teacher, on the Chart Holder while the class watches. When completed, the word is covered and children write on their papers.

2. The child at the Chart is asked to make the word into a *doing* word, which he does by adding the *ing* card.

The same child then writes the entire word on lines made by the teacher on the blackboard. The child who is writing cannot see the Chart Holder, but the class can. He names each letter aloud as it is written.

This is the place to make sure children understand how suffixes become part of the whole new word, with no space left between root word and suffix.

3. The class writes in the air, naming each letter as it is formed.

The word on the blackboard is erased. The one on the Chart Holder is covered.

Each child writes the word on his composition paper.

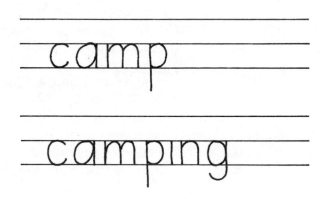

To show children how to check their own work, have each child cover *ing* with a finger, and look to see if the root word is just like the root word written above. In this way they can see their own omissions or mistakes, if any.

The teacher should check every child's paper before going to the next word. *Prevention, not correction at a later hour,* is vital to every teacher-directed step in structuring children's new learnings and experiences. The *quality, not the quantity,* of performance is the essential factor.

Each successive step depends on successful experiences and learning in previous steps. Individual sense of independent performance leads to a motivation that seeks "something harder" without fear of failing.

Continue in the same way for several lessons or until children have grasped the way to spell a root word that tells what we *do* and how to make it tell what we are *doing*.

*Fourth Step* — Leading to Greater Self-Dependence
Each child is given a sheet of composition paper.

1. A child is asked to work out orally, a word pronounced by the teacher, such as *mash*, (assuming the consonant digraph "*sh*" has been taught).

   The chosen child says: "Mash — /ă/, *a*, and repeats *mash*, and then spells orally, forming the letters with free arm swings.

2. The class names the word and writes *without watching hands* as arms form the letters. (The Chart Holder is not used and the word is not written on the blackboard.) Then the children write the word on their papers.

   The teacher moves about to give help where needed, to reform a poorly written letter for the child to trace, or to "okay" correct performance.

3. When finished, children are told to write, on the next line, the word that tells what we are *doing* when we *mash* something. A child will say *mashing*, and then all should write the word.

   The teacher should remind children to keep their letters close together and not to leave any space between *mash* and *ing*.

   The Alphabet Card on which *ing* appears should be in full view, and the teacher should write *ing* on the blackboard for it to be copied by any who may need this "crutch." Before long, this extra help will not be needed.

   A *Suffix Chart* can be started on which the teacher writes each suffix as it is taught. It is left throughout the year where it can be seen for easy reference. By the end of the first year it may or may not include the following suffixes, as shown below. This will depend on how fast the children are able to progress.

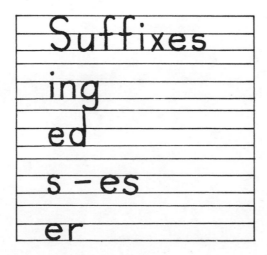

Continue in the same way with other words, first the root word, then on the next line, the root word with the suffix *ing*.

Later on, after Red Flag or non-phonetic words have been taught, adding suffixes that require no rules presents no problem when children have come to understand the "suffix concept."

Examples:

| | |
|---|---|
| want | walk |
| wanting | walking |

laugh
laughing

**Example 7 of a Daily Lesson Plan**

LEARNING TO WRITE

Each child is given 1" space composition paper.

The teacher dictates letters, consonant digraphs that already have been taught, and the suffix *ing,* such as:

p   h   t   j   m   f   sh   b   ck   w   ing

to be written by the children and traced over three or four times. The teacher should move about the room to make sure letters are correctly used and correctly formed, and placed. (Refer to page 75.)

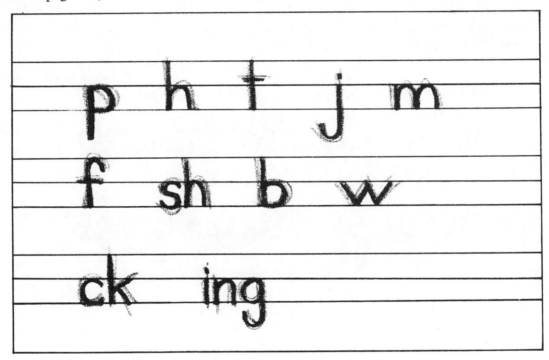

Procedure:

The teacher names a letter. Children write the letter, tracing over their own patterns. After several tracings, the teacher names the next one to be written without any time lapse between the completion of one letter and the beginning of the next. For digraphs, tell children to write the letters $s - h -$ /sh/ and for the suffix *ing,* write the suffix i – n – g, /ing/.

As already explained, the purpose is to help children develop a rhythmical movement from one "unit" to the next, something highly essential to successful written spelling and requiring an automatic auditory, visual kinesthetic-motor association for recall.

If some children, and there are always a few in any classroom, cannot move from one "unit" to the next as quickly and rhythmically as the majority, let them complete the one they are practicing and when finished, move to whatever letter is being named by the teacher, even if one or two letters are skipped. Give encouragement by telling these children it is better to do a few *well* than to try to hurry and fail. They will be able to accomplish more in time.

As this pattern of performance—intake-integration-output—with its auditory-visual-kinesthetic associations becomes securely fixed, the child gains momentum and the ability to move rhythmically from one letter to the next. Usually this is accomplished by midyear. Thus, the automatic letter formation becomes the functional skill required for success with written spelling and with writing phrases and short sentences which are introduced in the second half of the year.

A.   *Alphabet Cards* (Allow approximately 5 minutes)

1. Without exposing the card, the teacher gives the *sound* of a letter, consonant digraph, or the suffix *ing*.

2. An individual child: a. Names the letter or letters, writing with full arm swing; b. Names the key word; c. Gives the *sound*.

3. The teacher exposes the card for visual-auditory association and the class repeats.

Continue with as many cards as time allows.

B.   *Blending (Encoding)* (Allow from 5 to 10 minutes)

Following the same procedure as given on pages 93-94, give individual children turns to work out such words on the Chart Holder as shown below:

| if | it | mash | cast | tick | slid |
|----|----|------|------|------|------|
| brim | ship | click | wish | will | |

C.   *Spelling*

Each child is given 1" space composition paper.

Follow the *Third Step* (page 109-110) with such words as:

| pick | kick | cast |
|------|------|------|
| picking | kicking | casting |

No words that require doubling of the final consonant should be used; such as hit — hi*tt*ing.

The amount of time to be spent in any lesson must determine the number of words that can be written.

**Structuring Functional Use of Spelling** (Taught under C — Spelling in Daily Organization) – PHRASES

In beginning this new step, the teacher can point out to the children that they now can spell and write well enough to learn something "more like grown-ups can do." They are able to spell a word like *fish* and the same word with a suffix, *fishing,* which means they can spell and write two different words that tell something about themselves or someone else, such as, *can fish.* They could say that their father *can fish* or that I *can fish,* but all they need to write now will be two or three words, and later they will be able to write more.

To *prevent* mistakes, a child is asked to spell *"can,"* following the usual technique. The class repeats by saying:

*"Can, c-a-n,"* forming each letter with the arm for the gross motor movement to aid independent recall.

Have the word *fish* spelled in the same way.

The children are reminded to leave a two-finger space between *can* and *fish* when they write this phrase: *can fish.*

The children write, using no capitals or periods and the teacher checks to see that letters are written with correct letter-size relationship within the lines and in correct sequence.

If a child makes a mistake, encourage him to enclose the mistake with brackets or with parentheses marks, and to rewrite the word.

When the phrase is completed, the teacher can say:

"If your father *can fish,* what is he doing? — Yes, *fishing.* You can write the phrase *is fishing* on the next line."

A child is asked to spell *is* orally, and the class should repeat.

If no child can spell *is,* the teacher should write it on the blackboard for it to be copied. *Prevention* of mistakes to ensure correct performance whenever possible is desirable, especially in initial experiences.

The child writes the phrase, and the teacher should give immediate help wherever needed.

Whenever a word of common usage is written for it to be copied by the children, the teacher should include it frequently in future phrase writing so the repetition of its use helps to make it "stick." Some children often tell the teacher she "need not write it any more" because they remember. Others who do need to continue to copy can be told to do so. Those who can "remember" can be told not to look until after they have written the word, and then to check for correctness. The "crutch" should not be removed from those who continue to need it just because a few quick learners do not.

Other words can be used in phrasing. Some examples are shown below:

| | |
|---|---|
| sift | ask |
| sifting it | *was* asking |
| can sift it | is asking *me* |
| is sifting | asking and asking |

Before writing any phrase, the children should be asked how many words are in the phrase.

Also, (carried over from the Visual Approach — page 180 ) have children swing their arms from left to right as they repeat the phrase — *is asking me* — to feel its rhythm.

*Composition Paper*

Composition paper of ½ inch spacing is advisable when writing phrases and sentences. It is desirable for the phrases and sentences to take on the appearance of larger *units*—associated with their meaning. This is an advancing step, stretching outward from "single units" (letters) to "word units" (groups of letters), and then to "phrase units" (fragmentary meanings) and to "sentence units" (meaningful arrangement of words and phrases).

The smaller spaces allow the words of the phrases and sentences to be written so they appear as groups or *units of words* that *belong together.*

**Example 8 of a Daily Lesson Plan**

LEARNING TO WRITE

Review recently taught letters (as explained in Lesson 3 on page 98, and pages 73-74) and then introduce a new letter (as explained in Lesson 5 and on page 100).

AUDITORY APPROACH

A.  *Alphabet Cards*

Review all the letters that have been taught (as explained in Lesson 7 on page 113).

B.  *Blending*

Including the most recently taught consonants and vowels, have the children encode words and syllables on the Chart Holder as explained on page 94.

Words to be used should be listed in the teacher's Plan Book before the lesson begins, to make sure that the tempo of the class performance moves along without delay.

*Examples of Words or Syllables:*

| nab | pat | pin | pan | trip | gap | gasp | cash |
|-----|-----|-----|-----|------|-----|------|------|
| diz | daz | (*but not duz*, which could become confused with the real word *does.*) | | | | | |

C.  *Spelling*

*Each child* should have half inch composition paper.

*The teacher* should name a phonetic word such as *limp* and ask an individual child to "work it out" orally.

*The individual child* should do so by saying, "*Limp, /ĭ/, i, limp, l-i-m-p,*" forming each letter in the air as it is named.

*The class* should repeat the word and then:

Name and write each letter in the air as the word is *spelled orally*.
Write the word on their papers.

*The teacher* should ask another child to make *limp* into a "doing" word.

*The individual child* should say: "I will add *i-n-g.*"

*The class* should write *limping* under the root word *limp.* (Refer to page 110.)

*Phrases for Dictation*

| | |
|---|---|
| *was* limping | *was* should be written on the blackboard to be copied as the "red flag" word to be learned (page 121-124) or reviewed. |

must limp
is limping
will limp

Plan more phrases than there may be time to write. Some children may be able to accomplish more than others. A few children, however, may be able to do no more than a minimum. The teacher should keep in mind that this minimum, correctly done, will afford more learning and secure patterning for such children than failing because of an attempt to keep up with the class.

**Structuring More Functional Use of Spelling** (To be taught under C.—Spelling in the Daily Format) — Red Flag or Irregularly Spelled Words

Learning Non-phonetic (to the children) or Irregularly Spelled Words as "Wholes"

The teacher must guard against requiring children to learn too many words too fast. When the thought pattern of learning is secure, Specific Language Disability children begin to gather a faster momentum in perception, integration and recall.

The introduction of words "to be learned" comes about naturally in phrase writing. As an example, the phrase might be *was camping.* The non-phonetic word, *was,* must be learned "as a unit or whole."

The teacher writes *was* on the blackboard to be copied. *She always should check every child's performance to make sure words have been copied in correct letter sequence and letter formation.*

The teacher should explain to the children that *was* is a word *anybody* must learn as "a whole word" because it cannot be sounded out in the way they have learned to spell so many other words. Tell them that there will be other words to learn this same way, but they will be shown how to do so when it is time.

1. Children are told to say the word *was* to make sure they know what word they are practicing to learn.

2. They trace lightly over the word they have copied, *one letter after the other,* and name each letter aloud, but softly, as it is formed.

   Children continue to name the word and to trace until each child thinks he can remember.

3. To check themselves, children are shown how to close their eyes and to write the word in the air, naming and feeling each letter as it is formed. *If an arm hesitates or stops,* the child will know his head has forgotten and therefore, cannot direct his arm. This means he needs to practice more by tracing and naming the letter.

   Children should be reminded to feel the first sound of the word. This helps them to recall the first letters; e.g., "*was* — /w/ — *w.*"

   The purpose is not only to build behavior patterns of study, but to put some of the responsibility for learning on the children themselves. Children's basic urge to learn and to succeed provides strong motivation when they are shown *how* and are *not afraid to try* for fear of failure or condemnation.

Examples of words "to be learned" when needed in phrase writing:

*was* kicking                                    *was*

| | |
|---|---|
| can kick *out* | *out* |
| kicking out | |
| was kicking out | |
| *to* kick and kick | *to* |

| | |
|---|---|
| to mash it | |
| mashing it *up* | *up* |

Until such time as the vowel *u* is taught, the word *up* will have to be copied and "learned."

| | |
|---|---|
| *want* to mash | *want* |

If the teacher feels *want* is too difficult to learn at a given time, it can be used for copying alone.

| | |
|---|---|
| to *the* camp | *the* |
| camping out | |
| to *go* camping | *go* |
| *has* to camp | *has* |
| want to camp | |
| want to go camping | |

Repetitious copying of the word *want* often brings about learning without the child's realizing.

| | |
|---|---|
| *my* trick | *my* |
| tricking my cat | |
| *I* can trick | *I* |

The need to learn to write a capital letter comes about naturally in the last phrase given above.

*Teacher judgment must determine which words children CAN LEARN AT A GIVEN TIME and which can be copied, but not necessarily learned at the moment.* However, some children are able to learn faster than others, depending upon the degree of their disabilities. If they wish to study words that are intended for copying only, they should be permitted to do so if they already have learned securely the words that are required. Those who learn more slowly, again depending on the degree of the disability and individual "tempos" of moving and accomplishing given tasks, should be encouraged to learn *well* as many words as they can and no more at the moment.

*Phrase writing* and *how to study* particular words keeps children busy "on their own" for brief periods of time, while the teacher moves about giving help, encouragement and commendation. *It helps to avoid "behavior patterns of time wasting."*

It is recommended that a WORDS TO REMEMBER Chart be placed somewhere in the room for children's easy reference throughout the year. Words can be added to it from time to time as they are needed. The order of word placement on the chart may be entirely arbitrary.

| WORDS TO REMEMBER | |
|---|---|
| to | go |
| I | |
| was | |
| the | |
| want | |

To prevent mistakes, encourage children to refer to the Chart. They should be told that by writing words correctly without making any unnecessary mistakes, they become easier to avoid, and then they will not need to look at the WORDS TO REMEMBER Chart.

**Example 9 of a Daily Lesson Plan**

LEARNING TO WRITE

Dictate a letter or consonant digraph to be written in lower case. *Review* writing its capital form, or *teach* the capital if it is to be put to use in succeeding lessons.

Examples:   h-H   t-T   s-S   sh-Sh, etc.

AUDITORY APPROACH

A.   *Alphabet Cards*

*Example of cards* to use: t, m, c, f, g, j, sh, ck (/k/ as in jacks), etc.

*The teacher* should give the sound of a letter or consonant digraph.

*An individual child,* associating the sound with its visual symbol and name, should: name the letter while forming it in the air, name key word, give sound.

*The class* repeats, i.e. (if the letter is g) by saying "*g* — goat — /g/".

Continue by following the same procedure.

B.   *Blending*

Use the consonant digraph *sh.*

*Example word list* from which to select words:

| | | | | |
|---|---|---|---|---|
| ship | shift | dash | wish | shrug |
| sham | shaft | hush | fish | shrill |
| shut | shack | mash | flash | swish |
| shad | shall | sash | dish | swam |

*Individual children* should be asked to work out, orally, words named by the teacher (refer to Fourth Step, parts 1 and 2 on page 111) and then write on teacher-made lines on the blackboard.

*The class* should repeat the word and then write it in the air as each letter is named.

C.   *Spelling*

Each child should be given half inch composition paper.

*Examples* for phrase writing:

| | |
|---|---|
| she is | She is |
| swishing *them* | (*them* will probably be a "red flag" word until short e has been taught) |
| can swish them | |

The teacher should tell children when to use capital letters because they have no other way of knowing they should do so with phrases.

**Structuring Functional Use of Spelling** (Taught under C.—Spelling in Daily Format) — SENTENCES

SENTENCES — Use of Two or More "Phrase Units" to Make a Sentence or Complete Thought (Refer to page 144.)

*Step One* — Auditory — Practice in Verbalizing with Concept

The children should be told by the teacher that they are ready to begin to tell and to write something about the ideas they get from the phrases they have learned how to write. Some suggestions as to how to begin are given below:

1. The teacher tells the children that she will think of a phrase about someone or something and they can have turns to think of another that will complete the idea they get from what she says. She might say:

   "The little boy," and ask a child to add another phrase that tells something about him.

       The child might say:

       "had a bicycle."

   The teacher should say: "Yes, that told *what* he had. Now put the two phrases together—the one I said and the one you said." Give help, if needed, in verbalizing to make sure that the child can use both phrases.

   "The little boy had a bicycle."

   Continue in the same way, giving turns to different children to think of the final *one phrase* and to verbalize the complete thought or sentence.

2. Another suggestion is for the teacher to give the first "subject phrase," such as: "That toy," and ask different children to tell:

   *what* it does — with possible answers:

       walks by itself
       flies up high
       does tricks

*where* it *is* — with possible answers:

> on the table
> in the box
> where I put it

Each child should complete his turn by *verbalizing the whole sentence.*

3. Still another suggestion is for the teacher to take turns asking children to add the final phrase to her phrase: "The mother cooks," by telling *when* she cooks.

Children's possible answers might be:

> in the morning
> before dinner
> when we get home

The teacher can ask to have the same phrase, "The mother cooks" completed to make a sentence telling:

> *where* she cooks
> *for whom* she cooks
> *why* she cooks

Each child always should verbalize the entire sentence after giving the final phrase to complete the thought.

Children should be helped to *keep on the subject* and to stick to the one idea being used.

4. When familiar with the above "games," individual children should be given turns to think of the first phrase and to call upon a classmate to complete the sentence. One or both should verbalize the complete sentence.

5. Children can be given small pictures or objects about which they make a whole sentence while the class looks at the picture or object to see if the sentence includes a phrase *naming it,* and another *about it.*

*Step Two* — Writing Two Phrase "Units" to Make a Sentence

To start, make the sentences very simple. After children have written a root word with some of its suffixes and have used the same words in a phrase or two, put them together to make a sentence. Do not expect beginners to do more than one sentence in a lesson. From day to day others should be written but never too much at one time.

Examples:

She is⁀  ⁀wishing and wishing.

⁀He wished  ⁀for it.

⁀I have made  ⁀a wish.

The procedure is given in more detail below:

As an example, have the children write *he can run* (no capitals and no periods). Someone is asked to spell *he* aloud, as described in previous lessons — pages 116, 117, 118.

The class writes on their ½" space composition papers, and the teacher checks.

The children are asked what one word can tell *how* someone who can move quickly can run. Children may mention several ways, and when a child mentions *fast*, it should be pointed out that *fast* is a good word to use because they can spell it. They are told to write *fast* on the next line.

They are told that since they are able to write *he can run,* and *fast,* they will be able to put them together to make a sentence that tells about a little boy. Have someone say: "He can run fast."

The teacher explains about capitalizing the first letter of the first word in a sentence and writes *He* on the blackboard. Children should copy first with a free arm swing for the gross motor movement and then with their pencils on the same line where *fast* was written. (Refer to page 132.)

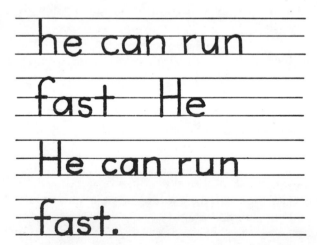

Children are told when they begin to write that they should begin on the next line, but first they should watch the teacher. She sweeps her arm to a pause after *run* as she says: *He can run,* and again after *fast.* The children should repeat in the same way to get the feeling for direction and the rhythm of phrasing.

If the teacher is facing the children *she* must be sure to swing her arm from *right to left* to prevent children's confusion from seeing a backwards (to them) sweep.

Have children tell how many words are in the first phrase (three) and how many complete the thought (one).

The teacher dictates *He can run.* When the majority are finished, dictate the last word *fast.*

Teach the children that a *period* is placed on the line after *fast* to show that the sentence is finished. (Periods should not look like pin points, nor should they be big and heavy like golf balls.)

As an example, when children have had more experience, use two phrases, such as: *He can run* and *to the crib.* The teacher can say: "Let's make believe that 'he' is your baby brother. Maybe he sees his crib, so *where* can he run?" – "Yes, *to the* crib." She says:

"He can run                         to the crib."

Have children sweep their arms to a pause at the end of each phrase as it is repeated.

As children write the first phrase from the teacher's dictation, the teacher should remind them about beginning with a capital letter and about leaving two finger spaces between words.

With SLD children, in these initial steps for organizing placement of words on their papers and for phrase concept, disregard indenting at the beginning of lines. This can be taught at a later date. They only need to return to the margin.

To aid in auditory recall when the teacher is dictating, if a child forgets and asks to have the last phrase repeated, *instead of telling him the phrase,* the teacher should remind the child that the first phrase tells that the baby *can run,* and the last one tells *where* he can run. This is often all that it takes to trigger a child's auditory recall of *to the crib.* The phrase and its meaning have been associated in previous discussions.

AN IMPORTANT REMINDER TO TEACHERS: The goal is for children to learn how to write the necessary phrases to express a complete thought. Therefore, it is essential not to place obstacles between the acquisition of "thought pattern" and performance. The phrases should not contain words so difficult to spell that children become confused to the extent they lose sentence concept. The teacher can write a new or difficult word on the blackboard for copying, something which they already have learned to do. (Pages 121-124.)

Some children will complete the sentence ahead of others. They can be told to begin on a new line—possibly on the back of the paper—and to write the sentence that the teacher will give them. It will have the same meaning, only it will begin *The baby can run,* instead of *He can run.* The teacher should write *The baby* on the blackboard to be copied.

These children can be reminded that after they finish and check their work, and are told that it is correctly done, they can study *The* and *baby* by tracing and practicing in the way they already have learned to do. This will help the more able to learn to spell and to study independently.

Children who are able to complete no more than the one sentence because their disabilities may be more extreme, should be commended for what they accomplish. They should be encouraged to practice any of the words they are not sure they can spell.

Discourage erasing in favor of putting brackets or parentheses marks around mistakes, and then rewriting correctly, if able to do so. Scratching out errors with pencil marks should not be part of acceptable standards.

Future explanations of the real meanings of brackets and parentheses can be given in higher grades when the need arises. For the present, all that the children need to know is that they explain to the teachers and to themselves that what is enclosed is a mistake, so recognized, and that an effort has been made to make a correction.

Erasing makes holes in papers and involves delay when erasers are misplaced, or when the necessary hand transference from pencil to eraser and back to pencil must be made. Crossing out mistakes usually results in untidy and messy appearing work. Another reason for no erasures is to enable the teacher to see the kinds of errors that are made. Then instruction can be directed to specific weaknesses.

The children are encouraged to *think before performing*. This performance pattern evolves when there is freedom from undue pressure for speed in favor of *thinking first,* with time allowance for recall before performance. The goal is to be able to write without making unnecessary errors. Then the brackets or parentheses will be needed less and less, if at all.

**Example 10 of a Daily Lesson Plan**

LEARNING TO WRITE

By the time children have reached this point, and if no new letter at this particular time is to be taught, functional use of already acquired penmanship skill can be carried directly into the different steps of the AUDITORY APPROACH. However, the LEARNING TO WRITE period *should be retained on a regular basis.* Beginners continue to need the security gained from practice and over-practice.

AUDITORY APPROACH

A. *Alphabet Cards*

Use 5 to 6 letters or consonant digraph sounds for transposing sound to written symbol. Examples: n, j, p, r, w, ck

Children should be given half inch composition paper.

*The teacher* should give the *sound* of the letter (naming the key word, if needed).

*An individual child* should: Name the letter, the key word, and give the sound.

*The class* should: Repeat the above procedure, write the letter on paper, and then trace lightly over each pattern.

The same procedure should be followed with the other letters.

B. *Blending*

Use 3 or 4 words. Examples: pant    will    and    run

*The teacher* should pronounce one of the words.

*An individual child* should encode orally in the usual way by repeating the word, giving the vowel sound, naming the vowel while forming it in the air, repeating the word again, and spelling it orally.

*The class* should repeat the word, spell orally and then write the word on paper. To help recall the word for future use, sometimes children should trace over their own word pattern after the teacher gives approval of its correctness.

The same procedure should be followed with the other words.

C.    *Spelling*

The back of the composition paper should be used.

Examples of phrases:    *he will    run and pant.*

*The teacher* should dictate first one phrase and then the other, reminding the children to tell themselves how many words are in the phrase.

Example of sentence: *He will    run and pant.*

*The teacher* should first say the whole sentence and then dictate each phrase. The children should be reminded to think about how sentences *begin,* and how they *end* when they tell something.

If necessary, give help with capital *h*. (Refer to page 128.)

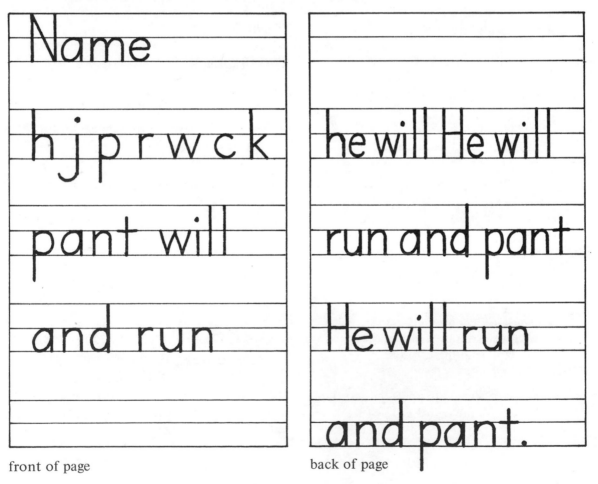

front of page                                   back of page

**Structuring the Use of the Suffix *ed* and the "Past Time" Concept**

*Step One* — Auditory — Concept-Verbalizing (Refer to page 108.)

The teacher says to the children: "If *camp* tells what I *do,* and *camping* tells what I am *doing,* how do you suppose I would use the same word, *camp,* to tell what I did *last summer* or *before right now?*"

As soon as a child says *camped,* or that he *camped last summer,* write the suffix *ed* on the blackboard for all to see, and place the Alphabet Card, on which *ed* appears, in the Chart Holder beside the suffix *ing* card. Remind them that they already know how to use the suffix *i-n-g* and how it gives a special meaning to the word *camp.* Tell the children that the suffix *e-d,* when added to the word *camp,* will give *camp* still another meaning.

Using either phonetic or non-phonetic words from a list, such as the one shown below, and *disregarding their spelling* and how they look, the teacher—if using the word *walk*— should say, "If *walk* tells what I *do,* and *walking,* what I am *doing,* how do I say what I *did* yesterday, or this morning, or before now?" Elicit the word *walked.*

Help different children to verbalize by having them say, "I *walked,*" or "I *walked* with my big brother," or in some other way.

If a child should say: "I walked with my friends," the teacher can elicit the "past time" concept by asking *when they walked — right now* or *before right now* or *at some time already gone by.*

A *suggested word list* to use to develop the concept:

| | | | | |
|---|---|---|---|---|
| ask | plan | help | tip | wait |
| skip | scream | trace | climb | scrub |
| snow | rain | smash | fish | wish |
| cover | plant | coast | nod | scramble* |

While developing concept, disregard entirely the fact that the suffix *ed* has three sounds—/ĕd/ as in planted, /d/ as in snowed, and /t/ as in camped. Not until the concept and use of *ed* is thoroughly understood need this be pointed out— probably not until the Second Year Continuum of this approach to teaching SLD children.

*If children are taught to spell by a phonetic approach alone,* they will probably spell *camped* with a t — campt. When these average to superior children gain the concept or learn "through the intellect," understanding becomes a strong factor in *preventing* this kind of error. Because some SLD children have difficulty recalling how words *look* and others, how they *sound,* they need to gain some

*Slingerland, *Teacher's Word Lists,* page 40.

means of depending upon themselves through their understanding. They need to be taught "suffix concept" much more carefully than do non-disability children whose auditory-visual associations are automatic, serving them with quick recall.

Add to the children's self-confidence by telling them that now they understand what "past time" means. They know two suffixes—*ing* and *ed*. Both will be left on the Chart Holder and on the Suffix Chart, and *when it is the right time*, they will be able to learn more.

Irregularly formed past tense words such as:

| | |
|---|---|
| go | went |
| sleep | slept |
| swim | swam |

should be taught as "wholes" if they are needed in any of their first year experiences in writing or verbalizing.

*Step Two* — Oral Spelling with Auditory-Visual Association When Words are Made on the Chart Holder (Refer to page 109.)

*Teach under B.—Blending in Daily Organization*

This provides children with an auditory-visual-motor experience in which they must move their hands to sequence the letters correctly without having to recall letter form for writing.

An individual child is given a turn to blend a root word (verb) on the Chart Holder, always following the same procedure as explained on page 79. When completed, the child and the class should spell orally, using arm swings to form each letter as it is named.

The same, or another child, should be asked to use the suffix that will make the word mean "past time." The *ed* card should be added and the whole word spelled orally again.

The *e* and the *d* are kept on one card so this suffix —*ed*, just as with the suffix *ing*, is learned as a unit or "whole"—not only as an aid for understanding suffixes, but also for visual recall.

  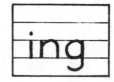

The children should verbalize in such ways as:

"I made (*root word*) mean past time."
"I put *e–d* to make (*root word*) say *(child pronounces the word.)*"

Cards should be replaced in their correct places on the Chart Holder before the next child is given a turn.

Refer to *Word List* on bottom of page 109.

*Step Three* — Written Spelling (Refer to bottom of page 109.) Auditory-Visual-Kinesthetic Association

*Teach under C.—Spelling in Daily Organization*

Follow the same procedure as given in Step Two, using the Chart Holder. After the child completes the word, he writes it from memory on lines on the blackboard. The class watches. The child should name each letter aloud as it is written, speaking for others to hear.

> If the child should forget how to spell the word after going to the blackboard, he should be told to blend it again and to *write* each letter as he names it. He should not return to the Chart Holder to see it. *This is done to help the children form behavior patterns of self-reliance and self-confidence.*

Before the class writes on its 1" space composition paper, the word on the blackboard should be erased and the one on the Chart Holder should be covered.

Children are asked to write the root word. On the next line they write the same word with the suffix. (Refer to page 109-110.)

Repeat the same procedure with other words in the daily lessons that follow.

*Step Four* — Written Spelling — Leading to Greater Self-Dependence

*Teach under C.—Spelling in the Daily Organization of Instruction*

Each child is given 1" space composition paper.

1. The teacher names a phonetic, one-syllable short vowel verb. (Refer to Word List on pages 109 and 139.) The class repeats the word.

2. An individual child blends the word orally (page 84), but does not use the Chart Holder or write on the blackboard.

   The class repeats, using arm swings as each letter is formed and named.

3. The class writes on its papers.

4. Have someone tell what should be done to make the word mean "past time." All the children should write on the next line. As they learned to do with the suffix *ing,* they should cover the suffix with a finger to see that the root word is like the root word above.

   Continue with other words from day to day until reasonable security in using the suffix *ed* is attained.

   Sometimes include both *ing* and *ed* in the same lesson.

Examples:  hunt        fish        land
           hunted      fishing     landed
           hunting     fished      landing

135

**Experiences to Reinforce and to Review Suffix Concept of** *"ing"* **and** *"ed"* **and for Verbalizing Answers to Teacher Questions**

To aid children to verbalize an answer to a question related to suffix concept, the teacher can say:

"How do we say the word *race* to make it become a 'doing' word?"

The child may answer "racing," which he is told is right, but it would be better to answer in a sentence by saying: "We say *racing*."

Verbal children usually have no difficulty, but for the non-verbal child, the teacher should "put the words into his mouth" for him to repeat. In time, such a child acquires a "thought pattern" for sentencing. (All through the elementary grades of schools with SLD Programs, children with verbal weaknesses frequently turn to their understanding SLD teachers to ask, "How would I say that?" Often no more than the introductory phrase triggers the release of words and phrases needed for the desired self-expression.)

Below are some suggestions for teacher questions or directives to which children answer in sentences or with just one word:

Teacher: "How do we use the root word *race* to tell what happened in the past—before right now?"
Child: "We say *raced*."
Teacher: "How do we use travel to make it tell what someone is doing?"
Child: "We say *traveling*."
Teacher Directive: "Make *travel* a past time word—a word that tells what we or someone *did* before now."
Child: "Traveled."
Teacher Directive: "Make *play* a *doing* word."
Child: "Playing."

*Another Suggestion*

The teacher picks up a picture (or object) and says:
  "I *look* at this picture right now."
She puts the picture aside and says:
  "Tell me what I *did* while I held the picture."
A child tells her:
  "You *looked* at the picture."
The teacher, taking up the picture again, asks:
  "What am I *doing* now?"
A child tells her:
  "You are *looking* at the picture."

*Another Suggestion for Understanding and Verbalizing Sentences*

Ask a child to perform some act, such as tapping, hopping, running, etc., and to "keep right on" performing while the teacher calls upon another child to tell what he is *doing*.

The child called upon says: "(Bobby) is (*hopping*)."

Have the child who performed the action stop and then ask another child to tell what he *did before he stopped*.

The answer could be: "You *hopped*."

Still another child should be asked to tell what the child who performed the action can *do*.

The answer would be: "He can *hop*," or "You can *hop*."

Continue in the same way by giving other children turns to show some action and others to verbalize answers to questions.

Such experiences lead to more success with written answers required of children as they advance into higher grades. Ability to verbalize orally frees them to concentrate on writing what they wish to express. Unless preparation for this need begins early, Specific Language Disability children often fail miserably when third and fourth year written work requirements cannot be met.

Creative and imaginative teachers relate action with its language to make these experiences seem like games and fun to the children.

**Structuring the Use of the Suffix _"er"_ to Form Nouns — "The Names of Persons and Things."**

Some first year children do not progress to this point while others do. The teacher must be the judge of whether or not to delay teaching the suffix _er_ until the Second Year Continuum.

Follow the same steps as already explained for _ing,_ page 108, and for _ed,_ page 133.

_Step One_ — Concept — Verbalizing Auditory-Kinesthetic (Speech) Association

1. Children will have learned that:

   > _jump_ tells what you _do._
   > _jumping_ tells what you are _doing._
   > _jumped_ tells what you _did._

   The word _jumper_ is elicited when they are asked to think what you are called when you jump.

2. As soon as the sound /er/ is heard at the end of jump, Alphabet Cards are placed beside the _ing_ and _ed_ Cards on the Chart Holder, the teacher adds _er_ to her pack of cards, and _er_ is written on the Suffix Chart.

   By now children will probably have gained "suffix concept."

A suggested _Word List_ of verbs from which nouns can be made:

| | | | | | |
|---|---|---|---|---|---|
| grab | clap | drill | nap | clamp | bake |
| pick | clip | pump | skate | drop | train |
| hug | nod | train | spin | run | tumble |
| rent | wash | laugh | talk | paint | ride |
| toast | groan | coax | pout | scoot | fly |
| scream | beg | draw | read | swim | hike |

Because no spelling or reading is required or presented, any verb can be used.

_Step Two_ — Oral Spelling with Auditory-Visual Association When Words are Made on the Chart Holder

_Teach Under B. — Blending in Daily Organization of Instruction_

This provides for auditory-visual-motor experience as children's hands move to correctly sequence the letters of the word on the Chart Holder without any need to recall letter forms for writing.

Individual children are given turns at the Chart Holder to blend phonetic, short-vowel, _one syllable verbs that require no doubling of the final consonant before adding a suffix._

They add the *er* Card to make *the name of the person or thing that can do what the root word indicates.*

*Suggested Word List*

| | | | | |
|------|-------|-------|--------|-------|
| kick | grasp | stamp | pass | twist |
| mash | clamp | trick | stick | lift |
| slash | limp | wish | drift | swish |
| wish | dust | hunt | splash | fish |
| pinch | snack | sift | clomp | smash |

*Step Three* — Written Spelling (Refer to pages 109-110 and 135). Auditory-Visual-Kinesthetic Association

*Teach Under C.—Spelling in the Daily Organization*

Follow the same procedures as given in Step Two, but by this time, a child, instead of using the Chart Holder, may be able to go directly to the blackboard to work out the root word orally, then to write it and add the suffix.

When the child finishes, all the children should pronounce the word and write with arm swings, naming each letter as it is formed.

The word is erased and children write on their papers.

Continue in the same way with other words.

> If any child *needs* the security he gains from working out the word on the Chart Holder first, he should be permitted to do so.

Use as many verbs with the suffix *er* as time and the children's ability for the moment permits in any one lesson.

In lessons that follow, review the use of other suffixes by including them.

As soon as a root word is written on paper, it can be used with the suffixes *ed* and *ing* without having each word written on the blackboard.

> Refer to page 110 for the way children should check their own work at the same time the teacher is moving about the room to give help and approval.

*Examples*

| | |
|---------|---------|
| pass | fish |
| passing | fisher |
| passed | fishing |
| passer | fished |

To be sure children understand the meaning suffixes put into words, the teacher should ask such questions as:

"What suffix must I add to make the word mean *past time*?"
"How will I make this word mean the *name* of somebody?"
"How can I make it tell what someone is *doing*?"

*Reminder to Teachers:* Some children may be able to accomplish more than others. If some can write no more than one root word with suffixes, and *be successful,* this is much better than attempting more than can be handled which means failure becomes the end result. At this stage, success is the goal—not speed or quantity.

*Step Four* – Written Spelling Leading to Greater Self-Reliance:
   *Teach Under C.—Spelling in Daily Organization of Instruction*
All children should be given composition paper.

The teacher should name the verb or "root word." A child should blend orally. The class should spell orally. Children should write the word on their papers.

The teacher should ask the children to write the same word on the next line and make it mean the *name* of a person (or thing). Before the children begin to write, a child should be asked to tell which suffix to use—*er*.

Continue with other words until reasonable security in using the suffix *er* is attained. Then include *ed* and *ing* for review.

*Examples*

| | |
|---|---|
| dust | swish |
| dusted | swisher |
| dusting | swishing |
| duster | swished |

In other lessons, use phrases and sentences.

*Examples*

| | |
|---|---|
| stick | will *get* a sticker |
| sticker | |
| is sticking | He will get a sticker |
| to stick to | |
| | |
| sift | sifting the *flour* (copied) |
| sifting | |
| sifter | She is sifting the flour. |
| sifted | |
| | I sifted the flour. |
| | |
| | *It* is in the sifter. |

**Structuring the Use of *s* and *es* as Third Person Singular Suffixes — With Concept**

This teaching may come after or before introduction of the suffixes *ed* and *er*. Its placement herein is arbitrary.

*Step One — Auditory — Verbalizing Concept*

*The teacher* should pronounce different verbs for individual children to use in telling about themselves—"*what I do*".

*Individual children* should say: "I walk," "I cry," "I paint," "I crawl," "I swim," etc.

Next, *the teacher* should pronounce different verbs, and ask individual children to tell *what others do* by eliciting from them—"You skip," "You swim," "You dream," "They walk," "The mothers (or they) sew," "The people (or they) work," "All the children (or we) run," "Airplanes fly," etc.

Then *the teacher* should direct children's attention to listening for what happens when they tell about *one other person or one other thing*. They should be asked to tell about *mother who can cook, the boy who can ride, the toy that can run,* etc.

Individual children should say: *Mother cooks,* or *The boy rides,* or *The toy runs,* etc.

If a child says, *"Mother cook,"* the teacher should ask if it would sound right to say that Mother *cook a pie for me every week.* If this fails to elicit the correct response, the teacher should tell the child to listen for the way that sounds better when she says it two different ways. She should say, *Mother cook a pie for me every week,* and *Mother cooks a pie for me every week.* Usually this serves the purpose, but if it does not, the teacher should say the sentence correctly and overemphasize the /s/ and then ask the child to repeat so he can "hear and feel" the right way—an auditory-kinesthetic association.

To give children further practice in verbalizing, such phrases as are shown above can be used to make whole sentences.

*Summarize* by having the children discover that sometimes the sound of an *s* is heard. They can tell:

1 by the way the word sounds when it is spoken, and
2. because it is needed when we talk about *one other person* (or thing).

The teacher should remember that many SLD children learn how to recall through their inherent ability to intellectualize. Such children have a Specific Language Disability—and *not a learning disability.*

An *s* should be placed on the Suffix Chart with the other suffixes that have already been learned.

*Word List:* (no reading or spelling is involved) For Teacher Reference only

| | | | | | |
|---|---|---|---|---|---|
| swim | hike | skip | jump | play | draw |
| write | scream | sleep | crawl | lift | climb |
| drop | wind | chain | creep | twist | grab |
| play | love | like | slide | hope | pick |

THE SAME PROCEDURE SHOULD BE FOLLOWED with es which has the sound /ĕz/. The *es* should be placed on the same line with the s on the Suffix Chart. (Refer to the Suffix Chart shown on page 111.)

*Word List:* (no reading or spelling is involved) For Teacher Reference only

| | | | | |
|---|---|---|---|---|
| fish | wash | catch | pinch | hatch |
| dish | buzz | dress | fix | pitch |
| hitch | fuss | pass | miss | mash |
| hush | dash | lunch | brush | touch |
| smash | trace | race | wish | lose |

*Step Two — Auditory-Visual Association and Motor Experience*
Verbs should be written on the blackboard or placed on the Chart Holder.

Each word should be named by the teacher or by a child (if the component parts have been learned in the VISUAL APPROACH — B.—Unlocking Words). *The teacher* should call upon individual children to answer her questions, using full sentences, by telling if s or es should be added or if no ending is needed. The children should add the s or es card to the word on the Chart Holder when necessary, or write the correct ending to the word on the blackboard.

*Example of a word list* with teacher *questions:*

| | | | | | |
|---|---|---|---|---|---|
| purr | crawl | read | swim | bark | pinch |

Pointing to, and reading one of the words, the teacher should ask someone to:

| | |
|---|---|
| Tell what cats do. | — Cats purr |
| Tell what the kitten does. | — The kitten purrs |
| Tell what your brother does. | — My brother swims |
| Tell what all the boys do. | — All the boys swim |
| Tell what you can do. | — I can read |
| Tell what the shoe does. | — The shoe pinches |
| Tell what the shoes do. | — The shoes pinch |
| Point to a friend and tell what he can do, etc. | — You can pinch |

When a word such as *race* is shown, the children should be told that only an s need be added because an *e* is already there to be with the s to make the sound /ĕz/.

Avoid using words that require a rule before adding the *s* or *es,* e.g., cry-cries, try-tries. This should be left for future learning and should not be injected at this time to cause possible visual confusion.

*Step Three* — Refer to Step Three in adding other suffixes on pages 109-110 and 139.
*Step Four* — Refer to Step Four in adding other suffixes on pages 111 and 140.

## D. – DICTATION – INTRODUCED IN 2ND YEAR CONTINUUM
## E. – CREATIVE WRITTEN EXPRESSION AND INDEPENDENT WORK

Children's creative written expression becomes a spontaneous outgrowth of learning how to spell, write phrases and sentences and to verbalize their thoughts. The desire to write independently usually follows sentence verbalizing, explained on pages 126-127.

As one example of what children do with paper such as that shown below:

they make a picture in the upper space and on the lines under the picture, a descriptive sentence is written.

To assist the children to organize their thoughts, the teacher should point out how they can help themselves.

1. *Think first* about the picture.
2. *Begin by writing a phrase, or a word,* that names what is in the picture.
3. *Finish the sentence* by telling something about it.
4. *Remember* the ways sentences begin and end.

Children soon find their own creative ways of self-expression through writing. Materials that might be needed should be left within easy reach or made available when requested.

Teachers can find innumerable suggestions of what has been and can be done in: *INDEPENDENT CREATIVE IDEAS FOR USE WITH SPECIFIC LANGUAGE DISABILITY CHILDREN.* Eldra O'Neal and Helen Zylstra, Cambridge, Mass., Educators Publishing Service, Inc., 1971.

### Summarizing Progress and Looking Ahead

Not all SLD children will progress at the same rate as do Non-SLD boys and girls. Some will not attain functional use of all that has been explained herein, as the general objective. They should be led forward from their final point of first year attainment when they begin the second year. Others may progress sufficiently well to continue on into the Second Year Continuum.

None of the steps can be hurried or hurdled without causing confusion to the children, for which reason it is essential that first and second year SLD teachers work together. Administration should not expect all children to be brought to the same level at a given TIME. EXPOSURE TO INSTRUCTION WITH PRECONCEIVED IDEAS OF WHAT ALL CHILDREN SHOULD HAVE LEARNED AT A GIVEN TIME IS MORE APT TO PER-PETUATE DISABILITY THAN PREVENT IT.

*In general, the First Year Continuum* of new learning includes:

### LEARNING TO WRITE
— letter forms as an auditory-visual kinesthetic association
— letter forms for rhythmic movement from one letter to the next
— recall of letter form for functional use in spelling and written expression.

### A – ALPHABET CARDS
— probably most of the consonants by the year's end,
— at least three short vowels—*a, i, u,* probably *o,* and possibly *e,* but only if the others have become functional,
— probably the consonant digraphs—*ck, sh, ch, wh, th.*

### B – BLENDING*
— phonetic, one-syllable, short vowel words containing the vowels *a, i, u,* probably *o,* and possibly *e,*
— phonetic verbs with suffixes *ing, ed, er,* and possibly *s* and *es* for third person singular verbs.

### C – SPELLING
— Green Flag words—phonetic words of one syllable with short vowels *a, i, u* probably *o,* and possibly *e,*
— Red Flag words—words to be *learned* for recall,
— suffixes *ing, ed, er,* added to both phonetic and learned verbs,
— NO RULES.

### D – DICTATION
— phrase writing,
— short sentences,
— (dictation for paragraph concept is introduced in the Second Year Continuum).
*Slingerland, *Teacher's Word Lists.*

E – INDEPENDENT AND CREATIVE WRITING
- Refer to page 144, and to
- *INDEPENDENT CREATIVE IDEAS FOR USE WITH SPECIFIC LANGUAGE DISABILITY CHILDREN\**

*Looking ahead to the Second Year Continuum,* new learnings will include:

## LEARNING TO WRITE
- continued experience with letter forms as an auditory-visual-kinesthetic association
- practice with letter forms to bring about automatic functional use in recognition, spelling and written expression
- capital letters.

## A – ALPHABET CARDS
- frequent review of all consonants and short vowel sounds *a, i, u, o,* and short *e.*
- many diphthongs, vowel digraphs, phonograms,
- vowel-consonant–e (v-e)–*a-e, e-e, i-e, o-e, u-e,*
- consonant digraphs, such as kn, ph, etc.

## B – BLENDING\*\*
- short vowel words,
- vowel-consonant-e words,
- words whose vowel sounds are spelled with more than one letter, such as *ow*–/ō/,/ou/, and *igh*–/ī/, etc.,
- phonetic words with suffixes,
- letter combinations, such as *ank, ing, ung,* etc.,
- some phonetic two-syllable words.

## C – SPELLING\*\*
- Green Flag words–phonetic words,
- Red Flag words–words to be *learned* for recall.
- Yellow Flag words–words containing ambiguously spelled vowel sounds or consonant sounds,
- more suffixes, with concept, such as *ful, able, ness,* etc., and further development of the suffix *s* or *es* for third person, singular verbs,
- singular and plural,
- words with letter combinations such as *ing, ank, ung, tion,* etc.,
- NO RULES.

\*O'Neal, and Zylstra, *Independent Creative Ideas.*
\*\*Slingerland, *Teacher's Word Lists.*

## D – DICTATION
– paragraph writing, with concept, introduced and structured with functional use of all that is taught in the above areas.

## E – CREATIVE AND INDEPENDENT PROPOSITIONAL WRITTEN EXPRESSION*
– creative stories or other individually planned self-expression,
– how to write answers to simple questions.

*Ibid., page 146.

# PART 4

THE VISUAL APPROACH FOR READING

## THE VISUAL APPROACH FOR READING

Refer to pages:
3 through 8
9 through 12
14-15
24 through 31

## THE VISUAL APPROACH

**Procedures**
(Refer to pages 37-40.)

Just as with non-disability children, screening\* can indicate that some Specific Language Disability children are ready to begin reading immediately, while others are not.

Some children may need delay with emphasis given to activities and non-reading developmental language experiences to foster concept-verbalizing abilities\*\* before any attempts are undertaken to superimpose visual, or graphic, symbolic language.

When a group of Specific Language Disability children is deemed ready to begin learning to read, each day's lesson plan should be structured and presented within the *Visual Approach* at a time entirely separate from the lessons planned within the *Auditory Approach.* (Refer to page 37.)

Suggestions to use with children for their independent constructive and meaningful activity while the teacher is giving the preparation and guidance in reading to one of the several reading groups are plentifully supplied in INDEPENDENT CREATIVE IDEAS FOR USE WITH SPECIFIC LANGUAGE DISABILITY CHILDREN, by Eldra O'Neal and Helen Zylstra, Educators Publishing Service, Inc.

### A.   ALPHABET CARDS

Because all the children in an SLD class should begin with a single unit of sight-sound-feel in the LEARNING TO WRITE period, all can take part at the same time in the drill to strengthen recognition of consonants and vowels and their association with sound.

### B.   UNLOCKING WORDS

Unlocking words (decoding) should be postponed until blending (encoding) for spelling, taught in the *Auditory Approach* becomes reasonably automatic and functional. (Refer to pages 77-85.)

---

\*Beth H. Slingerland, *Pre-reading Screening Procedures,* Cambridge, Mass., Educators Publishing Service, Inc., 1969.

\*\*Slingerland, *Training in Some Prerequisites for Beginning Reading.*

C.   PREPARATION FOR READING

For the groups *ready to begin to read*, refer to pages 174-185.

For those in *need of delay*, devote this block of time to visual-motor and auditory-motor experiences which include verbalizing each activity with teacher assistance and reinforcement.

D.   READING FROM A BOOK

Reading from the material for which preparation is given—under C—PREPARATION FOR READING—should be carefully structured as explained on pages 185-199.

For the temporarily "delayed" children, continue verbalization, using pictures and environmental activities and other material to develop readiness for reading.

E.   THE GOAL

In the beginning, no more than success at the instructional level under teacher guidance should be expected, but as children's vocabulary can be recalled, reading of material below the instructional level should be encouraged.

Material at a level below instructional level should be placed where children can use it for independent reading.

Below is the daily organization to serve as a guide for structuring daily lessons in the VISUAL APPROACH:

---

### DAILY ORGANIZATION FOR INSTRUCTION

> LEARNING TO WRITE (Refer to pages 40 – 49.)
> This is part of the AUDITORY APPROACH, *not* the VISUAL APPROACH

| THE AUDITORY APPROACH | THE VISUAL APPROACH |
|---|---|
| (Refer to page 56 and page 77.) | **A.  ALPHABET CARDS**<br>Refer to pages 154-157.<br><br>The teacher should expose the card and the child should:<br>1. *Name* the letter while forming it in the air,<br>2. *Name* the key word,<br>3. Give the *sound*. |
| | **B.  UNLOCKING (decoding) PHONETIC WORDS**<br>Refer to pages 157-174.<br><br>*Unlocking should be delayed until blending for spelling (AUDITORY APPROACH) has been taught* to enable children to understand how "word wholes" are formed from "single units". This will become a time for:<br>1. Teaching something new, and,<br>2. review and practice. |
| | **C.  PREPARATION FOR READING**<br>Refer to pages 174-185. |
| | **D.  READING FROM A BOOK**<br>Refer to pages 185-199.<br>This follows the preparation as given above. |
| | **E.  THE GOAL**<br>Independent reading of material below instructional level. |

153

## LEARNING TO WRITE

The grapheme-phoneme auditory, visual, kinesthetic-motor association needed for learning to write should be taught and practiced during the LEARNING TO WRITE periods that should precede and lead into the AUDITORY APPROACH. (Refer to pages 39-49 and 49-52.) This "learning" enables children to follow sequential steps required for functional use in spelling (Auditory Approach) and for letter recognition in reading (Visual Approach).

## A.   ALPHABET CARDS

From the teacher's pack of Alphabet Cards, those letters that have been taught in the LEARNING TO WRITE period should be withdrawn to make a separate pack *for use with the children.* As new letters are taught, their cards should be added to this "functional" pack which, by the end of the second year's continuum of instruction, usually contains all the consonants, vowels, digraphs, dipthongs, letter combinations and phonograms. (Refer to pages 28, 29.)

The teacher's pack of Alphabet Cards should contain the same cards that appear on the Chart Holder. (Refer to pages 24, 49 through 52.)

In the *Visual Approach* the initial stimulus, as it appears on the Alphabet Card, is *seen* and *nothing is heard.* This is opposite to the Auditory Approach in which the initial stimulus is *heard* and *nothing* is seen.

When a letter (or letters) is *seen* and perceived, it is conceptualized and associated with its sound and "feel" before it is spoken orally.

Children should have daily practice and review with as many as can be used in the 5-10 minutes devoted to this drill to strengthen automatic recognition and association.

## STRUCTURING THE USE OF THE ALPHABET CARDS

In the beginning, there may be only one or two letters to use, but even so, follow the procedure as given below:

1. *The teacher* should expose one of the cards.

2. *An individual child* should be asked to "tell about this letter."

As soon as children understand what is expected, the teacher should do no more than expose a card without saying anything more because the child should know what to do.

With the first few letters the teacher may need to guide the child through each step until his "thought pattern" becomes automatic; that is, by telling the child to: 1) *Name the letter and form it in the air as it is named*, 2) *name the key word*, and 3) *give the sound.* If a child hesitates with recall of the key word, encourage him to *look at the Wall Card.* Sometimes recall of the name of letters is triggered

154

by telling a child to keep forming the letter in the air until its name pops into his mind. Give a child *time to think* through each step so his "thought pattern" becomes "fixed". Often, to trigger recall, the teacher need do no more than say—"Name", or "Key Word", or "Sound".

*The child's automatic response* should be to:

1. *Name* the letter while forming it in the air with a full arm swing from the shoulder,
2. *name* the key word, and
3. give the *sound.*

3. The entire class should repeat.

Another letter should be exposed. Several children should be given turns with each letter to enable every individual child to have a turn to perform *as an individual.*

In time this practice moves smoothly from one card to the next with the teacher saying almost nothing unless an individual needs extra help or a new letter needs extra practice.

Children should not be asked or allowed to watch their hands while the letters are being formed in the air. This arm swing is purely for the strengthening of gross motor movement and kinesthetic recall of the letter's "feel" in association with its name and sound.

155

*Variation in Practice*

1. A child should be asked to go to the Chart Holder, to select one of the Alphabet Cards and place it clearly apart from the other cards to make it stand out for all to see, and then to "tell about" this letter in the same way as explained on previous page.

   Other children should be given turns.

2. After the children have learned to form the letters accurately during the LEARNING TO WRITE period, *a child* should be asked to go to the blackboard and to write a letter of his own selection on lines made by the teacher.

   When finished he should choose another child to "tell about the letter I made."

   *The chosen child* should *name* and form the letter in the air, *name* the key word, and give the *sound*.

   *The class* should repeat.

   This is not the time for children to write on paper. Writing practice should be done during the LEARNING TO WRITE and AUDITORY APPROACH periods.

## B.   UNLOCKING WORDS (decoding)*

This block of time should be *used daily for teaching something new or for review.* After something new has been taught—a vowel or a diphthong, etc.—it should be included with previous learnings for review and practice to afford the repetition SLD children require.

### STRUCTURING THE FIRST USE OF CONSONANTS FOR UNLOCKING WORDS

In the beginning, no attempt should be made to have the children try to unlock whole words because they will not have had time to learn enough letters, and because the blending build-up of single "units" to make "whole word units" should be introduced through the AUDITORY APPROACH. (Refer to pages 77-85.) After concept for and practice in *blending* "whole words" is understood and reasonably functional, the *unlocking* of words should be introduced thorugh the VISUAL APPROACH. Until such time, usually about the second semester, the teacher should move directly from A—ALPHABET CARDS to C—PREPARATION FOR READING and D—READING FROM A BOOK (refer to page 153) when planning the daily lessons. However, as soon as several consonants have been learned and appear on *Wall Cards* and the *Chart Holder* where children can refer to them, they should be used in initial steps toward learning how to unlock words—as explained below.

*Use of Single Consonants in Initial Steps*

A list of words that 1) *have been taught and practiced during* C—PREPARATION FOR READING, and 2) contain some words that begin with any of the consonants already learned during the AUDITORY APPROACH and LEARNING TO WRITE periods, should be placed on the blackboard.

*In this Visual Approach* with its *auditory-kinesthetic association*, the teacher should explain to the children that each word begins with the same sound that is made by the first letter. To focus on this letter, a line should be drawn under it.

1. *The teacher* should ask a child to draw a line under the first letter of the first word in the list and "tell about" the letter.

2. *The individual child* should:

   1) *Name* the letter while forming it in the air,
   2) *Name* the key word,
   3) Give the *sound* of the consonant,
   4) Pronounce the word to *feel* how it begins.

3. *The entire group* should repeat the word.

*To unlock or decode phonetic words for independent silent or oral reading, the children learn how to sequence correctly  the sight, or graphic, symbols in association with their auditory or sound counterparts.

157

The same procedure should be followed with each succeeding word enabling different children to have turns.

When the time comes for children to learn to unlock whole words, they may or may not omit naming the key word. This will depend upon the children's readiness to do so.

This same approach should be used during D−READING FROM A BOOK. If a child fails to recognize a word that begins with a previously learned consonant, such as *look*, the teacher should say:

"You know how to make the first sound which can help you to remember the word."

Time should be allowed for the child to think and to say:

"*L*, (forming *l* in the air), *lamp*, /l/."

Because the reading vocabulary is limited at this stage, just to *feel* the first sound often triggers recall of the whole word. Sometimes by prolonging the sound /l/, as a reinforcement to recall of the word *look*, confusion with a word of similar meaning such as *see* can be prevented and the child is more apt to say:

"look"

If recall does not occur, the teacher should tell the child to make the first sound, and she will complete the word for him to repeat. Another way would be to say that the word "tells what you do with your eyes," or "has a meaning something like the word *see*," to relate concept to phonetic skill.

To help the child who struggles to recall the name of the first letter, the teacher should say, "Keep forming that first letter with your arm because your arm sometimes helps you remember the name when you *feel* it. Look at the key word on the wall." If this fails to call forth recall, the child should be told to give the *sound* of what he *feels* and *sees*. Often the missing link in this three-way association is completed. Otherwise, the teacher should tell the child the name of the letter, and have him *repeat* the name while it is being *formed*. Then the child can do what he set out to do at the board where he underlined the first letter. (Refer to page 157, 158.)

*To use an Auditory Approach* with its *visual-kinesthetic association*, the teacher should explain that the children should *listen* for the first sound they hear in a word to be pronounced for them. To find the word, they should look for one beginning with the letter that makes that sound.

*A child* should be asked to stand to the side, with his back to the list of words, but not where the view of the group is blocked. *The class* should be able to see the words, but *the child* should not.

1. *The teacher* should *point to and read a word* from the list for the class to see as the child's performance is followed.

2. *The child*, with his back to the list of words and to the other children, should:

   1) *Repeat* the word named by the teacher—*loudly enough for* all to hear and for him to *feel and hear*.
   2) Give the *first sound* of the word, *not the name*.
   3) *Name* and "tell about" the letter—*name, key word, sound.*
   4) Go to the list of words to find and point (with a pointer) to the correct word and then, pronounce it.

   This serves as *an initial step for skimming* because children should be encouraged to run the pointer down the column of words until one beginning with the desired letter is located.

   *To require greater discrimination*, the list of words should contain more than one word beginning with the same letter. Some of the words may contain first letters whose sounds have not been taught. This, too, requires discrimination because children should skip over them, knowing they have not been presented.

3. The group should repeat the word pronounced by the child unless of course, the wrong word should be selected. The silence of the group indicates to the child that self-correction should be made, if possible.

4. *Other children* should be given turns.

The above "game" is not meant to be a teaching device. It provides variation in review, practice with what has already been learned, and pleasant repetition.

STRUCTURING A NEW LEARNING—UNLOCKING ONE-SYLLABLE, SHORT VOWEL, PHONETIC WORDS
(Refer to bottom of page 84.)

By the time SLD children are ready to learn how to unlock one-syllable, short vowel, phonetic words for reading, they should have learned (during the LEARNING TO WRITE and AUDITORY APPROACH periods) how to blend single units of sound—*letters*—into larger units of sound—*words*—which convey meanings that single letters do not. (Refer to pages 79-80.)

To unlock a word, children should begin with a "whole word unit" *that can be seen* and transpose its single units into sounds that, when resynthesized, give a "whole word unit" that *can be heard* and (to be hoped), understood.

Unlike in B—Blending, of the AUDITORY APPROACH, where the initial stimuli are auditory, in B—UNLOCKING, of the VISUAL APPROACH, the initial stimuli are visual. (Refer to page 197.)

| *Auditory Approach* | *Visual Approach* |
|---|---|
| To blend, the child *hears* (or thinks inwardly) the word, and then: | To unlock, the child *sees* and then: |
| 1) The word is *repeated*. | 1) The vowel is *named* and formed in the air. |
| 2) The *vowel sound* is given. | 2) The key word is named. |
| 3) The vowel is *named*. | 3) The vowel *sound* is given. |
| 4) The word is *spelled*. | 4) The word is *pronounced.* |

*DISCUSSION* should precede the introduction of unlocking phonetic words. Before this is undertaken the children—during the AUDITORY APPROACH, B—Blending, pages 77-85—should have come to understand how single letters with their individual sounds, grouped together in different ways, make words that can be seen and understood when they are written.

The children are told that everyone must *learn* some words by using them over and over in games and in reading—just as they have been doing (C—PREPARATION FOR READING, and D—READING FROM A BOOK) but now they are ready to do something harder. They know how to change sounds into letters that make a word that *can be seen when it is written*. By reversing the procedure, they are ready to change a group of letters into a *word sound that can be heard and understood*. They will be able to work out some words without help from anyone—after they learn how.

*The Chart Holder*, on which are displayed the consonants that have been learned, should be placed before the children. Only one vowel, *a*, should be used until the "thought pattern" for "unlocking" is *well established*.

Because "unlocking" should not begin until the second semester and *never* before use of the vowel *a* for blending is reasonably secure, enough consonants should have been taught to enable the teacher to make numerous one-syllable, phonetic words.*

*The Initial Procedure—with Short vowel a*
(Refer to page 79.)

The initial procedure is structured step-by-step so "unlocking" is learned letter-by-letter. Children should be reminded to think what every word must have to "open the throat"— *a vowel.*

1. *The teacher* should make a word, such as *lap*, with Alphabet Cards on the Chart Holder.

2. *An individual child* should be asked to point to the first letter, *l*, and name and tell about it in the usual way, by saying:

   "*l*, (forming *l* in the air), *lamp*, /l/."

3. *The teacher* should say:

   "The next letter is the vowel whose sound will open your throat. Tell about the *a*."

4. *The child* should say:

   "*a, apple*, /ă/."

5. *The teacher* should say:

   "Now make the sound of the *l*, and while you are saying /l/, think of the way your throat opens to make the vowel sound, and put them together."

6. *The child* should say: "/lă/."

7. *The teacher* should tell the child to work out the last letter, *p*, and to complete the word.

8. *The child* should say: "/lă/—/p/, *lap*."

Different children should be given turns to provide each child with an opportunity to gain confidence in his ability and to be given the kind of individual help that may be required from the teacher.

*Slingerland, *Teacher's Word Lists* and *Phonetic Word Lists.*

161

*The teacher* can help the child who has difficulty putting sounds together 1) by soundlessly blending the letters for the child to watch the necessary throat and mouth movement before trying to do so alone; 2) by telling the child to keep right on saying /lă̆/ until "his head" tells his mouth how the last letter *feels*, and then to complete the word with that sound; or 3) by giving the *meaning* of the word to call forth association of word meaning and phonetic skill so that the word can be named.

*Example of a simple word list* for the above procedure:

bat    tam    fad    dad    cab    wag    gas

*Shortening the Procedure* by moving immediately to the vowel
(Refer to pages 80-85.)

As soon as words can be unlocked, letter-by-letter, the procedure should be shortened by moving directly across the word to the vowel. The children should have come to understand, as the result of past experience, that the vowel and its sound provides the key to "working out" words. Therefore, their "thought pattern" should be:

1. To *name* the vowel,
2. To name the key word,
3. To give the vowel *sound*,
4. To pronounce the word.

A suggested *word list* containing short vowel *a*, the consonants b−c−f−g−h−k−l−m−n−p−s−t−w, and the consonant digraph ck.

| map | tab | gas | wag | ta*ck* | pal | gab |
|-----|-----|-----|-----|--------|------|------|
| mat | fag | tam | ham | pat | sack | back |
| man | lag | tab | am | at | an | |

1. *The teacher* should present a word such as *map*.

   Words may be made with Alphabet Cards on the Chart Holder or written by the teacher on the blackboard in a list (Some of the words can begin with a vowel.)

2. *An individual child* should run the pointer under the word until the vowel is reached or, if words are on the blackboard, draw a line under the vowel and say:

   *"a, apple, /ă̆/—map"*

As soon as vowel perception becomes automatic, no lines need be drawn under the vowel. When the key word is no longer needed, it, too, may be omitted, but this omission should not be rushed, often found to be needed right into the second year continuum.

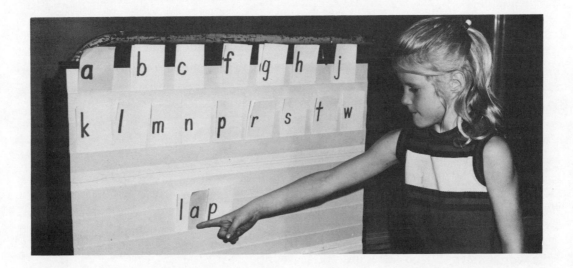

If a child needs to "work out" any consonant for recall of sound, encourage him to do so by referring to the Wall Card. *The child should be given time to think out the sound for himself.* The teacher already knows how and should not perform in place of the child. The teacher's role is to give guidance—not to do what the child should experience for his own learning in use of the "thought pattern".

UNLOCKING WORDS THAT END WITH MORE THAN ONE CONSONANT

Experience has shown that Specific Language Disability children learn to blend consonants that follow more readily than consonants that precede the vowel. Therefore, first experiences should begin with such words as those shown below:

| | | | | |
|---|---|---|---|---|
| lamp | mast | cast | ask | fast |
| raft | ant | damp | task | mask* |

*The same procedures* for unlocking words already explained on page 162 should be followed.

If a child omits one of the final consonants, help may be given in the following way:

In working out the word *mask*, *the child* might say:

"*a*, apple, /ă/—*mak*"

*The teacher* immediately should write *mak* and say:

"*This is what you said*, but you can see it does not look like this." She should point to the word—*mask*. "What letter did you leave out?"

*The child* should name the omitted letter, give its sound, and, if possible, make the self-correction needed. (Then the letters *mak* should be erased by the teacher leaving only the correct word to be seen.)

If difficulty persists, *the teacher* should cover the *k* while *the child* blends *mas* and then completes the word by adding the *k* sound.

*The child* after receiving special help, should be given opportunity to work out the same word again in order that *his final performance is one of success*—to enhance self-confidence and to strengthen use of the technique.

*Slingerland, *Phonetic Word Lists*.

UNLOCKING ONE-SYLLABLE, PHONETIC WORDS WITH SHORT i
(Refer to pages 90-93.)

The children should be reminded that they already know how to *spell* and write words with the vowel *i*, and, because they know how to *read* words with the vowel *a*, they can also use the vowel *i* for reading. They should follow the same "thought pattern" by:

1. *Naming the vowel* and forming it in the air,
2. *Naming* the key word,
3. *Giving* the *vowel sound*,
4. *Pronouncing* the word.

A suggested *word list* made with short *i*, the consonants b–c–f–g–h–k–l–m–p–r–s–t–w, and the consonant digraphs ck–sh–th (as in *thimble*) from which words may be selected follows:

| | | | | | | |
|---|---|---|---|---|---|---|
| bit | li*ck* | him | si*ck* | list | wisp | *thick* |
| jip | jib | hit | *sh*ip | rift | sift | wi*th* |
| tim | sip | wig | wi*sh* | fill | will | tilt |
| rib | fit | miss | di*sh** | | | |

*The teacher* should indicate a word to be worked out, such as *bit*.

*The child* should:

1. Name the vowel, forming it in the air—*i*
2. Name the key word—*Indian*
3. Give the vowel sound—/ĭ/
4. Pronounce the word—*bit*

*The group of children* should repeat the word—*bit*

*Other children* should be given turns in order that all, with daily practice, strengthen their automatic use of the "thought pattern" which leads to eventual quick recognition of short *i* words.

*Ibid., page 2.
Slingerland, *Teacher's Word Lists,* page 7.

A NEW LEARNING—DISCRIMINATION OF SHORT VOWELS a AND i
(Refer to pages 93-98.)

After children have learned to discriminate short vowel sounds *a* and *i* for *blending to spell*, they should be ready to discriminate these vowels *for reading*—probably by February of the school year.

A suggested *word list* from which words can be selected:

| | | | | | |
|------|------|------|------|------|------|
| fat  | fit  | wilt | tick | gab  | sham |
| dish | bag  | raft | pack | rig  | wig  |
| sag  | him  | list | map  | dash | wag  |
| ham  | last | lip  | path | cast | risk |
| *th*ick | tab | fish | lip  | task | fist |

*The teacher* should suggest that one child after another have turns.

*An individual child* should point to the vowel *a* in the word *fat* and say:

1.  *a* — forming it in the air.
2. apple,
3. /ă/,
4. *fat.*

The next child should point to the vowel *i* in *dish*, and, following the same procedure:

1. Name the vowel          — *i*
2. Name the key word     — *Indian*
3. Give the vowel sound   — /ĭ/
4. Pronounce the word    — *dish*

The teacher should make sure children are perceiving the consonant digraphs as "wholes". If evidence of individual weakness is shown, that child should draw lines under the digraphs for reinforcement of visual perception until they are securely "fixed".

As each new vowel is presented, the children should be given practice with it alone before using it for discrimination. As soon as its use becomes reasonably functional in unlocking words, it should be included with other vowels for practice and review.

## UNLOCKING WORDS THAT BEGIN WITH MORE THAN ONE CONSONANT

*"Consonant blends"* usually fall into place if previous steps in unlocking have been followed. *They need not be placed on Alphabet Cards* for drill in isolation. It is advisable for them to be perceived as part of a "whole word".

For teaching children this next new learning, a suggested *word and syllable list* is given below:

| | | | | | |
|---|---|---|---|---|---|
| slap | trick | grab | flat | spin | twin |
| slim | trip | grass | flit | span | twisp |
| slip | tram | grill | flap | spick | twill |
| slam | track | grim | flash | spill | twit |
| slash | trash | grasp | flag | spam | twig |

The initial step with a word such as *slap* should be for *the teacher* to call children's attention to the two consonants *s l* at the beginning of the word and to explain how *all the letters up to the first vowel* "go together". *Their sounds must be blended together before the throat opens for the vowel sound.*

*Procedure*

1. *The teacher* should ask a child to *name all the letters up to the first vowel*—using such a word as *slap*, for an example. They should name the letters—*s l*—and blend their sounds together and "hold" or "keep on making their sound". They should be told *or even shown*, how the first consonants must be "held" together before the throat opens for the vowel sound.

   *An individual child* should name *s l* and then blend them to say /sl/—prolonging the sound of the *l*.

   The teacher should be sure the vowel sound /ŭ/ is not allowed to follow the /sl/ because *sl does not say* /slŭ/.

   *Other children* should be given opportunity to find and blend only the letters that precede the vowel.

2. In the next procedure, the teacher should say:

   "From now on we will work out each *whole word* exactly as you already have learned to do.

   Look across the word, (or run your fingers *under* the letters, *not on them*) until you find the vowel. Tell about the vowel, and then pronounce the word."

*Do not have children draw lines under the consonant blends—only under what makes vowel sounds, when needed in a new learning.*

The children should be reminded to prolong the *sl* sound until *their heads* tell their throats how to open on the vowel sound before adding the last sound (or sounds) to complete the word.

*An individual child,* if using a word such as *trap,* should look across or run his finger under the *tr,* and stop at the vowel *a* to say:

"*a,* apple /ă/

trăp–*trap* "

If one of the first two letters is omitted, the teacher should write what was said in order that the omitted letter can be perceived by the child. (Refer to page 164.)

*The class* should pronounce the word—*trap.*

*Other children* should have individual turns to enable the teacher to give the kind of help each one requires.

It is advisable to give several words that begin with the same consonant blend before going immediately to another. After several blends have been learned, children should be *ready for discrimination* in words with different consonant beginnings.

From these experiences, SLD children soon learn to cope independently with other beginning consonant blends. *If they cannot, the teacher may have tried to hurry the children's learning,* or there is need for still more specific help and guidance.

## A NEW LEARNING–UNLOCKING ONE-SYLLABLE WORDS CONTAINING VOWEL DIGRAPHS, DIPHTHONGS AND PHONOGRAMS

### TO THE TEACHER

The number of short vowels that first-year-children can handle functionally depends on the maturity and the degree of the disabilities of the group. Often it has been deemed advisable by experienced SLD teachers to postpone the use of short *e* until the second year of instruction rather than to allow possible confusion between *i* and *e* to occur. However, a few of the vowel digraphs, diphthongs and phonograms may be introduced near the end of the first year *for reading*, after short vowels have been learned. Selections can be made from among these that are easy to learn, such as *ee, ou, oa, ar, er,* and possibly *oo* with its two sounds /o͞o/ and /o͝o/.*

The teacher should keep in mind that introduction and use of vowel digraphs, diphthongs, and phonograms *for reading* should move ahead much faster than *for spelling* because less recall is involved.

*For reading*, only perception of the vowel digraph, diphthong or phonogram in association with its sound is necessary for unlocking the word. The "unlocked" word adds to the meaning of the passage being read and reading continues with no further delay, whereas, *for spelling*, a much more complicated kind of perception, recall and memory is required.

*For spelling*, the word must be heard and retained in memory and the *vowel sound* must be perceived and discriminated from a background of other sounds before it can be visualized. Furthermore, the vowel sound may be spelled in one of several ways—e.g., *cream* has the vowel sound /ē/, but whether to use *ee, ea,* or *e-e* must be recalled or determined by asking the teacher (an initial step toward dictionary use). Letter sequence must be exact. Therefore, as soon as spelling becomes ambiguous, the number of vowel digraphs, diphthongs and phonograms that can be presented *for reading* outnumbers those that can be used in blending *for spelling*.

*Children* should not be expected to use the terms vowel digraph or diphthong or even to understand their differences in meaning. All such units of sight and sound can be called *"phonograms"*.**

### Procedures

*Exactly the same "thought pattern"* for unlocking short vowel words of one syllable is used. The child, already knowing how to seek the vowel *letter* that "opens the throat", need only perceive the *letters* of the vowel digraph, diphthong or phonogram and to 1) name them; 2) name the key word; 3) give the vowel sound, and 4) pronounce the word.

*Slingerland, *Phonetic Word Lists,* pages 14, 15, 16, 18, 19.
**Slingerland, *Teacher's Word Lists,* pages 21, 22, 23, 26, 30.

*The teacher* should expose an Alphabet Card,–e.g., *ee*–name the two letters, name the key word–*feet*–and give the vowel sound /ē/. *An explanation* about how two letters together often give the vowel sound should *prepare children for this new kind of perception.*

It is *better not to tell* children that the first letter of a vowel digraph or diphthong–"Phonogram"–says its name, and the next one is silent because this only leads to confusion–e.g., *ou* usually says /ou/ and not /ō/; *oi* says /oi/; *ea* can say /ĕ/ and /ā/, as well as /ē/; and *oo* says /o͞o/ and /o͝o/, almost never saying /ō/. EACH ONE SHOULD BE LEARNED FOR INSTANT PERCEPTION AS A VISUAL UNIT IN ASSOCIATION WITH ITS VOWEL SOUND TO OPEN THE THROAT.

*The teacher* should give many children turns to "tell about" a "phonogram" when it is introduced. The new phonogram Alphabet Card should be included in the Teacher's Pack for visual exposure in the daily review and in practice with Alphabet Cards.

*For children's practice* in learning a vowel digraph, such as *ee*, a list of "*ee* words"* should be placed on the blackboard.

| deep | feed | sheet | keep | meet | weed |
| beep | jeep | sleet | tweet | beets | weep |
| heel | cheer | teeth | wheel | keel | week |

*The teacher* should ask an individual child 1) to look for the letters that make the vowel sound, 2) to draw a line under them, and 3) to work out the word.

*The child*, after drawing the line under *ee* in *deep*, should say:

1. "*e e* (forming the letters in the air)
2. feet
3. /ē/
4. *deep*"

*Slingerland, *Phonetic Word Lists,* page 14.

As a preventive measure, any child apt to confuse b's and d's should be reminded at the outset to make the first letter of the word—which would be *d*, in *deep*—with his arm to let the "feel" tell whether it is *b* or *d*. (Refer to pages 62-65.)

*The class* should repeat the word—*deep*.

Other children should be given turns—especially those who may not volunteer, but *would like to perform* if given encouragement. Even some pressure to try with teacher guidance may be helpful.

Help should go to every child in need by giving guidance through each step, and *not by asking another child to perform for the one who falters*. SLD children have shown remarkable qualities of patience and understanding for each other's weaknesses.

Sometimes a child immediately recognizes a word without needing to work it out, at which time the teacher should say, "Good. Now work it out as if you had not recognized it, to give yourself practice in how to think through each step when you come to a word you don't know. Also, you are helping the others."

For some children it is advisable to present meaningless words or syllables, necessitating the use of the unlocking technique.*

*To The Teacher*

Lines need not be drawn under the phonograms and vowels after they can be perceived readily.

Each time *a new "phonogram"* is taught, children should be given practice with many words in which it appears *before* it is included with other words for vowel discrimination in a list of words such as the one below:

| | | | | |
|------|------|------|-------|------|
| peel | band | need | week  | spot |
| clash| park | club | punch | must |
| cart | coat | seem | slip  | harm |

A short period of practice and review for *unlocking* should be included in each daily plan of the VISUAL APPROACH before the Reading periods.

*Phonetic Word Lists for Children's Use* can be put into the children's hands near the end of the first year to provide opportunity for them to have turns to read words designated by the teacher from appropriate lists.

Vowel-consonant-e (silent-e) words, and much greater use of vowel digraphs, diphthongs and phonograms for both Reading and Spelling are presented in the Second Year

*Ibid., page 9.

Continuum. *Unless second year children have had a first year of preventive instruction, they will be unprepared to follow in this continuum until they are retrained by the same techniques used with beginners.*

## READING

Reading can be introduced at the same time it is presented in regular conventionally taught classrooms. Experienced teachers in most any classroom arrange children in groups—usually three groups—to meet their levels of "intake", and this same group organization holds true for Specific Language Disability classes. Just as in regular classrooms, some groups will be able to progress faster than others, for which reason daily lesson plans probably will be different for each group.

BECAUSE BEGINNERS WILL NOT HAVE FAILED, THIS APPROACH IS PREVENTIVE RATHER THAN REMEDIAL OR CORRECTIVE.

It is assumed herein that, at the outset, the primary teacher of those with SLD, like the primary teacher of non-SLD children, will spend some time in discussing the pictures and characters that relate to the material to be used, and that the teacher will include in *her* speech many of the same words that are going to appear in print. *However, this kind of motivation should be minimized in favor of a day-by-day emphasis on "over-teaching" words and phrases with their fragmentary meaning, in preparation for structuring the actual reading of these words and phrases within sentences—against a background of other words on a page—that convey the "whole" meaning.* Teacher help and guidance should be divided into two distinct areas of instruction:

C – PREPARATION FOR READING

D – READING FROM A BOOK

Specific Language Disability beginners want to read as much as do other intelligent Non-Disability boys and girls. *Successful performance, not just the desire to read, provides the motivation.* Unfortunately, it is the DESIRE AND INABILITY THAT INDUCES FRUSTRATION LEADING TO FEAR OR FAILURE OR RESISTANCE TO LEARNING. Therefore, *it is the teacher's task to provide the preparatory steps that bring about initial success, and a "learning" that is recognized by the children as stemming from within themselves*, when the books are placed in their hands. Their own success-learning induces the inner motivation that carries them forward with anticipation and offers its own satisfying rewards.

Use of a basic reading series* is recommended rather than highly programmed reading material because the conventional basic "readers" lend themselves to application of this technique better than material designed for its own phonetic approach.

*Scott-Foresman, Ginn, Houghton Mifflin, Bank Street, etc.

## C.   PREPARATION FOR READING—WORDS AND PHRASES

Preparation for reading always should precede reading from the book. The children first may look at the story to be read, but as soon as preparatory instruction is to begin, the books should be withdrawn and not left in the children's hands.

*The four structured steps* to foster recognition and recall of reading vocabulary, with concept, to be explained more fully, are as follows:

1. Teacher names; children repeat,
2. Teacher names; child finds and repeats,
3. Teacher gives meaning; child finds and reads,
4. Child reads; group repeats.

*Preparation* includes practice with *single words*—"word units"—and with *phrases*—"phrase units" that give fragmentary ideas, but not with both word drill and phrase drill in the same lesson (for lack of time).

While following the four steps of this teaching technique, practice with *single words* should be used at the outset as a starter for "fixing" a sight vocabulary, and always in *succeeding lessons* that may contain difficult or numerous new words.

The same four steps are used with *phrases* as soon as a few words of common usage can be recognized. Then, in succeeding lessons, new words often can be introduced within the phrase practice.

*Review and practice* of hard-to-remember words always should be included in daily lesson plans for either word or phrase drill.

If the words are *on cards*, they should be placed on a Chart Holder (not the one where Alphabet Cards are kept). If written *on the blackboard*, this should be done in well formed manuscript with the thick side of the chalk so that each word can be seen without any eye strain whatsoever.

Letters of one line should not overlap letters of another.

Children should be seated in such a way that they do not see words from an extreme angle or have to turn around in their chairs in order to see.

Space should be left between children and the blackboard or Chart Holder to allow for their unhindered movement to and from.

FOR WORD RECOGNITION

When teaching and giving practice with single words, no more than 6 to 8 (even less at the outset) should be taken from the material to be read.

Step 1—an *auditory*-visual-kinesthetic association

*The teacher*, placing and keeping the pointer under the first word, should pronounce the word clearly.

*The group* of children should *repeat* the word.

*Individual children* should be asked to repeat to enable the teacher to detect which ones need help with pronounciation.

*The teacher* should continue in the same way with each word. The meaning of some words should be explained or enriched, if needed.

The procedure should be repeated, skipping around the word list to make sure the children have *seen* and *heard* and *felt* each word as it is repeated.

This drill affords an auditory-visual association to which the kinesthetic is added as words are repeated. *The children* hear the word as it is clearly and correctly spoken by the teacher. *The teacher* can tell if children, performing individually, can recall the "feeling" of the spoken word within their speech mechanism. *Some children* have no difficulty, but others with auditory-kinesthetic disabilities may need immediate help with pronunciation.

(Refer to page 180.)

Step 2—to strengthen auditory-visual-kinesthetic association *and recall*

*THIS STEP NEVER SHOULD BE OMITTED OR SHORTENED WITH SLD CHILDREN although it is seldom required with Non-SLD children.* The initial stimulus is *auditory*—to be associated with the visual-kinesthetic.

*An individual child* should be given the pointer and asked to go up to the word list.

*The teacher* should name *any one* of the words.

*The individual child* should:

1. *Find* and *point* to the word, keeping the pointer *under or at the side of the word* to enable the group of children to see, and

2. *name* the word.

*The group of children* should repeat, *unless* the wrong word is indicated. By the group's silence, the performing child should know a mistake was made and, if possible, make his own correction. If any child in the group repeats an incorrectly named word, that child "gets caught" because either he was not sure of the word or he was not paying attention.

*Individual children* should be given turns to find and name different words *pronounced by the teacher.*

This affords auditory-visual-kinesthetic (A-V-K) association leading to secure recall. Children should not be expected to recall the names of words in association with their visual symbols until much practice has been provided in this Step 2. They 1) hear the word pronounced correctly by the teacher; 2) associate the sound of the word with its corresponding visual symbols; and 3) "feel" the movement of speech needed in kinesthetic-motor recall.

As soon as children understand the procedure, each child having a turn should be given two or three words to find. The practice should move along at a good, uninterrupted tempo or rhythm, and the teacher should do no more than name the words that are to be found and pronounced by a child and repeated by the entire group.

Step 3—to associate concept with word recognition. The initial stimulus is *auditory-concept,* associated with visual-kinesthetic

The teacher should give the *meaning of any one of the words*, but should not name it. For example, if the word list contains such words as *soon, play, Tom, Susan, happy,* and *home*, a child should be asked to *find and name* the word that tells:

"*the name* of the little girl"–(Susan)
"*what* the children *do*"–(play)
"*how* someone felt"–(happy)
"*where* mother *went*"–(home)
"*when* grandmother is coming"–(soon)

The *group of children* should be told that it will have turns to *find words whose meaning the teacher will give*, and to keep the pointer under each word until after it is *read*, and the class has *repeated*.

The *teacher* should say:

"Find a word that tells *where* mother *went.*"

*An individual child* should place the pointer under or by the word and say:

"home"

*The group* should repeat—unless, of course, the wrong word is named.

*The teacher*, as soon as children understand the procedure, should give *no more than the meaning* so that practice can move along at a good tempo. As an example:

"Find—*how* someone *felt*."

*The child* should point to the word and read:

"happy"

*The group* should repeat:

"happy"

*The teacher*:

"*when* grandmother is coming"

*The child*:

"soon"

*The teacher*:

"*what* children like to *do*"

*A child*:

"play"

*The group*:

"play"

Different children should be given turns. Children who hesitate to volunteer should be called upon because they usually want to perform even when they hesitate.

If the group of children make too many mistakes to allow a rhythmic and reasonably automatic performance as each word meaning is given for children to find and name the word, it may mean that not enough practice was devoted to previous experience with Steps 1 and 2, especially Step 2. Occasionally a child can point out the word with an understanding of its meaning but fails to recall the *name* of the word. This is one reason not to slight Step 2 because, in this step, the word is *heard* when the teacher pronounces it clearly and the child is given practice in making the association with its *visual* counterpart and its *feeling* when it is repeated.

This Step 3 is in advance of Steps 1 and 2 because *the teacher does not name the word*. Children must make the associations *from word meaning alone* before recalls can function. DEVELOPING AN UNDERSTANDING FOR WORD MEANING FROM THE MOMENT READING IS INTRODUCED, IS AN ESSENTIAL INITIAL STEP TOWARD PURPOSEFUL AND ENJOYABLE READING EXPERIENCES OF THE FUTURE.

Step 4—to check the "goal" which is recognition of the words. The initial stimulus is *visual*—associated with auditory-kinesthetic and (to be hoped, as words become more difficult) word meaning. (Refer to page 184.)

*The teacher* should call upon one child after another to read a word for the group to repeat.

*Each child* always should keep the pointer under or by the word, to hold the group's focus of attention, and *read the word*.

*The group* should repeat.

As children become familiar with the procedure, one child should read several words, and *the group* should repeat after each one is read.

*When beginning this Step 4*, if the teacher thinks that the children know the words—judging from their performance in Steps 1, 2, and 3—the "check" should be to call upon the weakest child first. If that child succeeds in reading the list of words, it is reasonable to believe that the others also are ready to read from the book.

If more drill appears to be needed, the first turns should go to the children who have least difficulty with word recall. In this way the weaker ones are given more opportunity for practice before they are given their turns to read the words.

If all the children make too many mistakes, *the teacher probably has not given sufficient practice with the preceding steps*, or, as sometimes happens with inexperienced teachers, the material to be read is beyond children's instructional level.

From this preparatory instruction the children should be ready for structured guidance in reading from the book.

The words just practiced should be left in sight for easy reference while the children are reading from their books during the teacher-controlled lesson that should follow this preparation. (Refer to pages 151, 153, 185.)

## FOR PHRASE RECOGNITION

When using "phrase units" the teacher should use no more than 4—6 phrases selected from the material that is to be read by the children. The phrases should be written with the thick side of the chalk if placed on the blackboard, or a wide pen if written on tagboard. In either case, they should be in manuscript. As many as 8 phrases can be used, but too many are not recommended at first.

*The purpose* of having "phrase drill" is to build patterns of "phrase intake", understanding, and recall without requiring too much memory at one time. Intelligent SLD children soon begin to use this patterning for phrase concept when reading from their books after the structured guidance—to be explained in D—READING FROM A BOOK—is given.

The same procedure explained in the *four steps* of *For Word Recognition* should be followed. (Refer to pages 176-180.)

*Example* of phrases that could have been selected from a page or two of a story to be read by the children:

> The little boy     the little boy
> can see
> in the box
> to see the box
> very happy

Step 1—an auditory-visual-kinesthetic association with concept. The initial stimulus is *auditory*.

This step provides a time for children to *hear* the phrases as they are associated with their corresponding visual symbols, and to *feel* the words in their speech organs as they are repeated.

*The teacher*, while keeping the length of the pointer under each phrase, should read the phrase rhythmically and in a conversational manner, *not word by word*. The rhythmical patterning should be demonstrated by sweeping the arm in an arc from *left to right* at the same time the phrase is being spoken, e.g.: (Refer to page 117.)

$\overparen{in\ the\ box}$   not   $\overparen{in}$   $\overparen{the}$   $\overparen{box}$

*The children* should repeat each phrase after it is read by the teacher. They, too, should speak in the same conversational rhythm, *not word by word*, and sweep their arms from *left to right*—"the way we read"—as the phrases are being repeated. (Refer to page 186.)

Here is a place to detect a child whose arm sweeps from right to left, rather than from left to right. Immediate help should be given to anyone showing confusion with the "feel" for *left to right*—"out from my body", for the right-handed child and "across my body", for the left-handed one. (Refer to pages 62-63.)

*The teacher* should begin to "intellectualize" the meaning of phrases by pointing out the way in which groups of words, *called phrases*, give *ideas* about something, such as:

> *who* it is, or *who* they see, etc.,
> *how* he felt, or *how* he ran, etc.,
> *where* someone or something is, etc.,
> *when* something happened, or someone is coming, etc.,
> *what* somebody did, or *what* they had, etc.,
> *why* something is done, or *why* someone hurries, etc.,
> *which* it is, etc.

Step 2—to strengthen auditory-visual-kinesthetic association, *and recall.* Its initial stimulus is *auditory*.

THIS STEP NEVER SHOULD BE OMITTED OR MINIMIZED. It provides needed practice for:

1. *hearing* the phrases correctly and rhythmically spoken, and *associating* them with their corresponding visual symbols.

2. experiencing the *kinesthetic* "feel" and rhythm of the phrases in the speech organs when they are repeated, and

3. developing eye span.

*The teacher* should tell the children to listen to the phrase as it is being said. Then, *one of them* will have a turn to 1) find the phrase; 2) put the pointer *under* it, and 3) read the phrase aloud. *The group* should repeat but not until the child finishes reading. The pointer should be left under the phrase to hold the focus of attention.

*The teacher* should say:

> "Find—*can see*"

*An individual child* should find and place the pointer under the phrase, and read:

> "can see"

*The group* (but not the child whose hand is holding the pointer) should repeat, sweeping their arms in arcs to "feel" the rhythm.

Arms automatically stop if a word is not recognized. This helps a child tell himself wherein his weakness lies and to concentrate on the spot in need of improvement or help. (*Teachers* should not minimize the fact that these are normal to highly intelligent boys and girls who *want* to know how to help themselves and to perform as independently as do children without Specific Language Disability.)

*The same procedure* should be followed with all the phrases to allow each child to have one or more turns to find and repeat. This drill should continue until children are reasonably secure in *recognition and recall*.

Recognition is not always enough because naming the words in speech is equally necessary for verbalizing and accurate recall. (Refer to pages 176-178.)

Step 3—to associate concept with phrase recognition. The initial stimulus is *auditory-concept* associated with visual-kinesthetic.

*The teacher* should give *the meaning of any one of the phrases*, but should not read them. For example, if using phrases as shown on page 180, a child should be asked to *find and read* the phrase that tells:

"*what* someone can *do*"—(can see)
"*who* has a box"—(The little boy)
"*where* something is"—(in the box)
"*what* someone *wants*"—(to see the box)
"*how* someone felt"—(very happy)

*The group of children* should be told that they will have turns to find the phrases whose meanings the teacher will give, and to keep the pointer under each phrase until after reading it. The group will repeat.

*The teacher* should say:

"Find the phrase that tells *who* the story could be about."

*An individual child* should place the length of the pointer *under* the phrase and read:

"A little boy"

*The group* should repeat: (Unless the wrong phrase is read)

"A little boy"

*The teacher*, as soon as the procedure is understood, should give *no more than the meaning of the phrase*. Then practice can move along at a good tempo without the teacher doing too much talking, other than to say:

"Find—*what* he can *do*"

*A child*, pointing to the phrase:

"can see"

*The group*:

"can see"

*The teacher*:

"Find—*what* he *wants*"

*A child*:

"to see the box"

*The group*:

"to see the box"

*The same procedure* should be followed to give different children one or more turns.

If children make too many mistakes, it may mean that *word vocabulary* needs more "fixing", or that too little time was spent with Steps 1 and 2; *especially Step 2*.

Just as with *Step 3* of *For Word Recognition*, this *Step 3* is an advancement over Steps 1 and 2 because the teacher does not *read* the phrases. Children must make the *association from phrase meaning alone before recalls can function*. Even more than the understanding of word meaning, phrase meaning is an essential initial step toward purposeful and enjoyable reading experiences.

Step 4—to check the "goal" which is recognition of the phrases. The initial stimulus is *visual*, associated with auditory-kinesthetic, and the meaning of the phrases.

Non-SLD children usually can go from Step 1 directly to Step 4 in which the initial stimulus is *visual*, but SLD children need the "over-teaching" and "over-learning" provided in the two intervening Steps 2 and 3 in which the initial stimulus is *auditory*.

*The teacher* should call upon one child after another to read a phrase.

*The child* always should keep the pointer under the phrase while reading to keep the group's attention held on the same point of focus, and it should be kept there until after the group responds.

*The group* should repeat, swinging their arms in an arc to feel the rhythm.

As children become familiar with the procedure, one child after another should read several phrases, and the group should repeat each phrase after it is read. (Refer to Step 4 of *For Word Meaning,* page 179.)

Step 4 demands only a short recall, but enough to prepare the way for strengthening recognition when these same phrases appear on the printed pages of the reading material which should be placed in the children's hands following this period of preparation.

Phrases should be left in sight for easy reference while the children are reading from their books during the teacher-controlled lesson that should follow this preparation.

## D.   READING FROM A BOOK

The reading material herein, used to illustrate structuring for reading from a book, has not been taken from any publication, but a good basic reading series* is recommended for classroom use.

No attempt has been made to present day-by-day plans for programmed progress. Examples of daily structured lesson planning are included, and they cover a spread of early reading levels—pages 199-231.

*"Preventive"* techniques to use with SLD children who are beginning to learn to read from the page of a book should be structured. Learning words and phrases within a controlled situation—as in C—PREPARATION—does not entail the same figure-background complexities of perception, recall, and cognition of the "whole thought" to be obtained from sentences, and in time, from the whole paragraph. Therefore, a part of each day's lesson should be devoted to structured *guidance in actual reading from the book.* (Refer to pages 151 and 153.)

Teachers should adapt procedures to material of their own selection, based on each group's, or individual's (if working with only one child) level of intake.

THE PURPOSE OF READING IS TO UNDERSTAND WHAT IS READ—NOT JUST TO NAME WORDS. THE SOONER THIS PATTERNING FOR RECOGNIZING WORDS AS CONVEYORS OF MEANING IS ESTABLISHED, THE BETTER FOR Specific Language Disability BOYS AND GIRLS WITH THEIR DISORGANIZED LANGUAGE PATTERNS. It takes a considerable amount of guidance and structured planning from the teacher.

*PRESSURE FOR SPEED READING SHOULD BE AVOIDED.* Fluency develops with ability to phrase and comprehend and unlock words, and until this is accomplished, SPEED SHOULD NOT BE EMPHASIZED. SLD children may never be speed readers; therefore, emphasis needs to be placed on independent use of reading skills and conceptualizing.

### Procedure for Structuring the Reading

Some teachers may prefer to have children place "markers" under the lines to be read. It has been found effective to have the *outer side of the hand* (little finger side) placed under the line. This relieves the children from holding (and dropping) the marker and from covering what should be exposed.

After preparation to read has been completed, the books should be placed in children's hands.

*The teacher* should tell how many words "go together" to make the first phrase in the sentence. As an example, with a sentence such as—"The red car is for Bobby"—she should say:

"The first three words stay together. Read them to yourselves."

*Scott-Foresman, Ginn, Houghton Mifflin, Bank Street, etc.

185

*The children* should be encouraged to sweep their arms in an arc to feel the rhythm. (Refer to page 180.)

*The group* should read to themselves.

Help should be given to show how to keep the side of the hand under the words. If markers are preferred, children should be taught how to hold them.

*An individual child* should read the phrase orally—in the same rhythmical speech that was practiced in Phrase Preparation. (Refer to page 180-182.)

"the red car"

*The teacher* again should tell how many words (possibly it might be only *one* word) "go together" in the next phrase because the phrase will tell *how,* or *who,* or *what,* or *when,* etc. She should say:

"The next three words will tell something about the car. Read them to yourselves."

*The group* should read silently while the teacher watches to see that all are keeping the place.

*An individual* child should read:

"is for Bobby"

*The teacher* should give a direction, such as:

"Now read the *two* words that tell exactly *who* the red car is for."
*An individual child*:

"for Bobby"

If a child says—"is for Bobby"—it should be pointed out that the direction given was to read only *two words*, not *three words*. This is to encourage *listening* and *comprehending* directions. The child should be allowed to make his own correction by reading the *two* words—*for Bobby.*

*The teacher* should ask someone to read the whole sentence.

"Read the whole sentence and remember to *pause* or *let your eyes rest* after you finish reading the word *car*, allowing time to see the next words that must *stay together* when you read them to us."

1. If the sentence is not rhythmically phrased, the child should be told: "You know the words. Now try again to read them as you would speak."

If the rhythm still is not *felt* and the reading continues word-by-word, the rhythm of the phrase should be tapped on the wall or table, or on the child's shoulder which is an even more effective way to emphasize accent. The child should try again, and sweep his arm as a reinforcement to the *feeling* of the rhythm.

2. Another suggestion with a phrase such as *the red car* is to ask:

"What thing is being spoken about—(*car*).

This helps to focus thought on the subject (or object) to assist in the association of comprehension and word recognition.

A *child's* next response to the question "*what kind of car?*" should be:

"red car" or "red"

Then *the teacher* should say:

"Yes, say it that way—just the way you talk."

Thus *the child* is helped to say:

"*the red car*" and not "*the red car*"

3. As a last resort, the teacher can read the phrase aloud and, at the same time, tap the correct rhythm on the child's shoulder. The child should repeat to the same rhythm as it again is tapped on his shoulder.

   The teacher should not "give up" because a child's first responses are less than desired. Succeeding lessons in which are different phrases, and continued guidance and casual encouragement usually bring about remarkable improvement and pleasure to the child.

*The teacher* should continue to guide the reading of other sentences until the page or paragraph is completed.

*A child* should be asked to read the whole page, or the paragraph, or the first two, or three, of four sentences.

If one of the sentences is poorly phrased, the teacher should not hesitate to have the child rephrase, always giving guidance to assist with comprehension and rhythm by:

1. Telling how many words "go together".
2. Naming the word on which to pause for eye span.
3. Saying that the phrase will tell *how*, or *when*, or *who*, or *what*, etc.

In this way, reading from a page is structured in order that both *learning* and *successful performance* go hand in hand. Even the child with extreme weaknesses is spared frustration when led through each step by the teacher's structured guidance. He is *prevented* from the fear of failure that often builds up into an emotional resistance to learning.

In the course of time, less structuring is required, but it *should not be dropped*. Only the *amount* should be modified and *the kind to be used* in a particular lesson should determine how the teacher's daily lesson planning should be made. When *something new* is taught in B—Unlocking, or in C—Preparation, it should be carried over into D—Reading for Functional Use. The teacher should avoid the assumption that this can be done by SLD children without structuring to bring about this *transference of a learning* into its *functional application*: to reading from a book.

**Procedures for Advancing Progress**

ASKING AND ANSWERING QUESTIONS–VERBALIZING

To be able to verbalize is necessary in all oral and written communication related to academic achievement and to daily life. Inability to verbalize what is read, even when there is comprehension, is a great handicap to SLD children (and adults). A *preventive measure* is to start early with simple questions giving guidance in structuring answers for children with this difficulty. *Telling* them to answer in a sentence is not always enough; they need to be *shown how*.

Something to avoid is asking a question that contains the answer because the child's "thinking ability" is not challenged. In a sentence such as:

THE LITTLE PONY RAN INTO THE BARN,

instead of asking *if the pony ran into the barn*, more thought is elicited if the question is worded:

"Where did it say the pony ran?"

*The child* probably would answer:

"into the barn"

*The teacher* should say:

"Yes, that is right, and to help you learn how to say that, give your answer in a complete sentence. Begin with a phrase that tells *what* you are talking about and then finish with a phrase that tells *where* the pony ran."

If some child has much difficulty, the teacher could say:

"I will say the first phrase for you—*the little pony ran* and you *repeat* what I say. Then finish with a phrase that tells *where* it ran."

The child should be encouraged to say the sentence over and to "sweep your arm as you say the first phrase, and then sweep your arm as you say the last phrase."

⌒ The little pony ran ⌒ into the barn

*The teacher* should point out to all children that:

"When we speak in sentences, we should think first of what we are *to talk about*, and then *say something* about that."

In a sentence such as:

MARY IS VERY HAPPY BECAUSE HER GRANDMOTHER IS COMING

even more thought is required when a question is worded to ask *why Mary is feeling as she does* than if it is worded: "*Is Mary happy*?". In this more involved question-answer—

*The teacher* should say:

"Think first of the person you will be talking about (Mary). Now start by saying *Mary* and then tell *how* she feels and *why* she feels that way."

*The child* would probably say:

"Mary is happy because Grandmother is coming."

"Mary is happy because *her* Grandmother is coming."

*The teacher* should not accept an incomplete sentence such as "happy because Grandmother is coming." *The child* should be asked to repeat the whole sentence again and to sweep his arm to indicate the phrases and to tell how many phrases were *felt*. It could be expressed,

"Grandmother is coming    and that    makes Mary happy."

THIS CONCEPT PREPARES THE WAY FOR WRITTEN EXPRESSION *BEFORE THE DAY ARRIVES* WHEN IT WILL BE EXPECTED, AND THEREFORE, IS PART OF THE "GLOBAL" STRUCTURING OF THIS APPROACH FOR TEACHING SPECIFIC LANGUAGE DISABILITY CHILDREN.

## PREVENTING b AND d CONFUSION IN READING

When children who continue to confuse *b*'s and *d*'s hesitate to pronounce a word, or they read one with b's or d's incorrectly, encourage them to "stop before guessing" and to look at the first stroke of the letter. Encourage them to put a finger directly under the letter.

*The teacher* should say:

"Form the letter in the air, and you can feel that it *begins with a tall stem* which tells you that is a *b*. When it *begins by moving round like an a,* you know it is *d.*" (Refer to pages 62-65.)

*The child* should form the first stroke and tell that his arm is making "a tall stem," or is "moving round like an *a.*"

More often than not, this visual-kinesthetic-auditory stimulus triggers correct recall of the letter, and the word itself may be recognized immediately.

Children's difficulty is seldom due to confusion with symbol-sound association, once *b* is perceived as *b*, or *d* as *d*. Therefore, as soon as the first stroke of the letter is perceived, this visual-kinesthetic-auditory association usually triggers correct recall, and discrimination becomes more automatic.

STUDYING ALOUD

When the children "study aloud" the teacher is able to catch, immediately, many confusions or errors or failure to recognize words correctly or to pronounce them right. The functional application of previous *learnings*, such as unlocking words, to the reading situation can be detected. In this way preventive help can be given at a time when it is most effective. By rereading after "studying aloud" children have the opportunity for *successful performance*.

The teacher should explain that each child will have a turn to study aloud while she and the group listen and learn.

*The teacher* should say to the child having the first turn:

"Read the first sentence aloud. Try to phrase the words by looking a little bit ahead before you say them. If they do not go together in the right way, you can read the sentence again. Then the phrases will be easier to keep together for their correct meanings."

*The child* should *read aloud* and then, to reinforce comprehension, rhythm and fluency, *read the sentence again*.

As reading ability progresses, an individual child can "study aloud" several sentences, or a paragraph, and then reread. When the "studying" of the whole paragraph or story by different children in the group is completed, the whole story should be reread orally.

Some questioning and answering should enrich the meaning during the "Studying aloud" time. *But group rereading of the story should be for pleasure and fluency alone.*

INDEPENDENT STUDY

By the time children reach first year readers (and the last part of primers sometimes, with more mature and rapidly progressing groups and possibly not until the second year) not all of the story need be structured.

After guidance through the first two or three paragraphs or pages, children should be able to study the final page or two by themselves—as they were shown how to do when "studying aloud." (Refer to page 192.)

After independent study, the group should return to read aloud to the teacher.

While they study, and do their assigned independent work,* the teacher should be free to help another group.

*O'Neal and Zylstra, *Independent Creative Ideas*.

PREPOSITIONS AND ARTICLES—Aids to Eye Span, Phrasing, and Concept

*Instruction* for these *new learnings* should be given during the periods devoted to *Preparation for Phrasing* (refer to pages 180-185), and when reading from a book is structured or "studied aloud."

*Independent use* of this technique by most children may not be possible until the second year, but many of the more mature first year children grasp the concept and begin to gain facility with its use before the first year is concluded. Independent use should not be expected until much guided experience has been provided.

The understanding and recognition of *prepositions* and *articles* assist in comprehending phrases and in developing eye span. After children's reading experience affords some familiarity with and recognition of *prepositions* such as *in, on, by, under, over,* etc., and the *articles the, a, an,* these small words will lend themselves to independent study and comprehension. One of the symptoms of weakness that SLD children show (noticed especially in Junior High, if not before) is disregard for and omission of small words. *Preventive measures* should begin early to develop awareness of the part they play in our language—hopefully, before children's placement in classrooms with Non-SLD boys and girls and the demands for speed reading override their ability to function under such pressure.

*In a discussion time*, children should be told that the little words are used to "tie together" or "cement together" other words that *name* what is being talked or read about. By "intellectualizing" this approach, and adapting it to any level of language achievement throughout the grades, intelligent SLD children often are quick to grasp the concept to be explained.

*The meanings* and *use* of prepositions and articles should be developed gradually in earlier reading lessons. After these words can be read easily, they can be used as a point of focus *before which eyes should pause* and then look ahead to the next words that "go together" to make a phrase.

Concept for prepositions as very important little words can be illustrated by placing on the blackboard a sentence such as:

TOM PUT THE CANDY IN HIS MOUTH

*The teacher* should read the sentence to the group and then say:

"What *one little word* tells *where* Tom put the candy?"

*An individual child* should name "in".

*The teacher* should ask a child to *draw a line under in,* and after the child draws the line, should say:

"Let's see how important this tiny little word is to the meaning of this sentence. See what funny things happen if I change *in* to another little word."

*The children* soon comprehend the distortion of meaning that occurs when the prepositions *under*, or *over*, or *by*, or *on*, etc., are used. They gain a concept for the need of prepositions to clarify meaning.

*The articles* should be described as little words that are *placed before other words that name something or somebody*. They tell our eyes to find the "name word". And they tell our eyes to pause just before we read them because they are *placed at the beginning of a phrase*. Phrases such as those shown below should be written on the blackboard:

a boy     an ant     the child
the cars     a house     an elephant

*The teacher* should explain to the children that they are to read the phrases, and when each one gets his turn, *a line is to be drawn under the first little word*. It tells us to look for the "name word."

*The first child* to have a turn should draw a line under *a*.

*Then the teacher*—to *help the child verbalize* his next performance—should say:

"Tell us where the word *a* (not pronounced /ā/) means for us to look."

*The child* should answer:

"*A* tells us to look for the *name word*."

*The teacher* should direct the child to read the *name word* and to draw a curved line—as shown below—and then to read the phrase so all can hear.

*a*  boy

Accent should be on *boy*, not on *a*.

*Other children* should be given turns with simple two-word phrases.

When children appear ready, concept for phrases that contain *adjectives* should begin to be developed. The *adjective concept* should be added to enable "describing" or "words that tell about" to take their place in the necessary eye span, and enrichment of phrase comprehension. The phrases shown below serve as examples:

*an* old animal
          *the* tiny, little bird

*An* and *the*, in the above phrases, alert the children to look for the *name words*; therefore, sweeping lines should be drawn accordingly. The children's *new learning* would be to note the intervening words and to discover their purpose—to "tell about" the *name word*.

195

For functional use of both prepositions and articles when reading from books, *the teacher*, at times, should:

1) point out the articles and prepositions in a sentence before which the eyes should pause;

2) remind children to reread a phrase or sentence when meaning is unclear;

3) discourage the rereading of a whole sentence in favor of reading the one phrase in need of improvement;

4) encourage children to keep together all the describing words until these words lead on to the name word. Then they should pause or reread the phrase.

*An example* of how to help those *who pause after*, rather than *before*, articles and prepositions is given below.

*The teacher* should write a sentence on the blackboard, such as:

MY NEW BOOK IS THE BEST ANIMAL BOOK I HAVE.

*The child* might read:

"My new book is the    best animal book    I have."

*The teacher* should say:

"You read—*my new book is the*. What is a *the*?"

*The child* usually catches his own incorrect phrasing; therefore, *he* should be allowed to make his own correction.

The skilled teacher soon learns not to spend a disproportionate amount of time in structuring, but, instead, to guide, illustrate, point out or answer questions that reinforce and confirm individual successful effort. Children should not be expected to learn everything in one or two lessons. Repetition and review in functional reading situations gradually brings about the desired self-dependence.

These learning activities serve as visual-auditory and kinesthetic-motor experiences associated with concept. When they are applied to functional use in the structured reading time, the teacher should remind children, at the outset of a lesson, to let their eyes pause before reading "the little words" they have learned about because they usually belong in the phrases that follow.

UNLOCKING WORDS

*Unlocking or decoding* one-syllable phonetic words is not introduced until *after blending* one-syllable words becomes reasonably functional for oral and written spelling. This decoding technique is usually introduced by the second half of the first year, (refer to pages 157 on) depending entirely on the time of the school year that academic work is introduced. It might come earlier, but it could be much later.

*Decoding* should be developed through a continuum of structured guidance, explained in B—UNLOCKING. After unlocking one-syllable, phonetic, short vowel words becomes reasonably functional, this skill should be carried over into reading from the pages of a book—for independent use—something that requires teacher guidance.

> *Children should not be expected to decode any phonetic word until its phonetic elements are known, even when there is the "thought pattern" for so doing.* (It is during the second year continuum that most of the diphthongs, vowel digraphs and phonograms, perceived as "wholes" for vowel sounds, and vowel-consonant-e, are introduced.)

When children hesitate in reading an unknown or unrecognized phonetic word whose phonetic elements already have been taught (and only the teacher knows which they are),

*the teacher* should say:

"You can work out the word. We will listen while you do."

*The child* should:

1) Name the vowel,
2) Give the vowel sound,
3) Pronounce the word,
4) Continue reading from the book.

> If first year children continue to need the security gained from naming the vowel while forming it in the air, and giving the key word, this should not be discouraged. Dropping this reinforcement too soon is discouraged.

When this decoding is beginning to be used while the child is reading from the book—

*the child* frequently asks:

"Can I do this word?"

If she knows the child is able to do so—

*the teacher* should answer:

"Yes, that is one you can work out by yourself."

If she knows the child has not yet learned its phonetic elements—as in the word *weigh*—

*the teacher* should say:

"No, you have not learned how just yet, but we will use it by and by in our *word practice* to help you remember," and then she tells what the word is.

*The teacher* might continue by saying:

"This word tells what you do when you get on the scales." (weigh yourself)

*Still another way* of giving help when a particular vowel has not been taught, is for *the teacher* to say:

"In this word (if the word were *crest*) I will tell what the vowel *e* says—/ĕ/, as in *elephant* which is all the help you need to work it out."

*The child* should say:

"*E*, elephant /ĕ/, *crest*"(and continue reading from the page on which he was studying).

Sometimes phonetic (to the child) words that are to appear in the reading lesson can be used in B–UNLOCKING of the Daily Lesson Plan, to reinforce recognition when they appear on the page.

*Example*

The word *swish* might be in the reading lesson. It could be placed at the top of a list of words to be unlocked by the children.

| | | |
|---|---|---|
| *swish* | fish | shift |
| dish | flash | shaft |
| wish | smash | swift |

The teacher, pointing to *swish*, should tell the children that this first word will be in the story they are going to read and that each child will have a turn to work out different words. During this practice, the teacher should return frequently to the word *swish* to reinforce recall and practice in unlocking.

**EXAMPLE 1 OF A TWO-DAY LESSON PLAN    PRE-PRIMER LEVEL**

FIRST DAY

VISUAL APPROACH

A.    ALPHABET CARDS

The Card Pack should contain letters already taught in the LEARNING TO WRITE and AUDITORY APPROACH periods and appearing on the Chart Holder. (Refer to pages 49-53.)

As an example the letters might be:

h    s    l    b    t    g    m    c    and    a

*Procedure*

*The teacher* should expose a card. (Refer to pages 52 and 154-157.)

*A child* should,

1) name the letter, while forming it with an arm swing,
2) name the key word,
3) give the sound.

*The group* should repeat.

*A child who needs extra practice* should be asked to repeat.

*Continue in the same way* with all the cards for several minutes, possibly going over them once or twice for all the children to have one or two turns.

READING

The reading material might be as follows:

IS A TOY A PET?

Bobby said, "See the *pony*.
See the little pony."

"The pony is a *toy*.
The pony is *my* toy.
See my toy," said Bobby.

"My pony is little," said Bobby.
"My pony is a toy.
See my little pony.
See my little toy pony."

*Conclusion of First Day's Lesson*

"My pony is a toy," Bobby said.
"I *can* play *with* my pony.
I play with my toy pony."

Bobby said, "The pony can *not* play.
The pony is a toy.
My pony is not a *pet*."

C.   PREPARATION FOR READING—For Word Recognition
(Refer to page 175.)

New words have been underlined.

*Word List* for practice: (The list should include both new and review words. For structured steps, refer to pages 176 through 179.)

| | | | |
|---|---|---|---|
| pony | with | | |
| little | my | ____ | My |
| toy | the | ____ | The |
| see | pet | ____ | Pet |

*Procedure*

*Step 1* (Refer to page 176.)

*The teacher* should point to and name the word *pony*.

*The children* should repeat *pony*.

*An individual child* who may need extra practice should be called upon to repeat.

The same procedure should be followed with each word.

When children are to learn a word in which the first letter will appear in both upper and lower case, it should be written in both ways enabling them to see the similarities and differences.

*Step 2* (Refer to pages 176-177.)

*The teacher* should name any one of the words, speaking clearly to make the last sounds clearly distinguishable.

*An individual child* should point with a pointer to the word, keeping the pointer under it while it is being read.

*The group* should repeat.

*The same procedure should be continued*, skipping around the list to give turns to all the children in the group. The words should be gone over several times for "over teaching" rather than "under teaching."

*Step 3* (Refer to pages 177-179.)

*The teacher* should give the *meaning* of any one of the words.

*An individual child* should *find and point* to the correct word and read it aloud so all can readily hear.

*The group* should repeat.

*The same procedure should be continued* with all the words, giving meanings, as suggested below:

"Show us a word that:

| | |
|---|---|
| — names an animal." | *pony* |
| — tells about, or describes someone or something." | *little* |
| — *you* use to say that something belongs to *you*." | *my* |
| — tells us to do something with our eyes." | *see* |
| — gives the idea of doing something together." | *with* |

"Show us three words (or as many words as you can) that are names of something."

> *pony*
> *toy*
> *pet*

Here is a place—with the word *pet*—to enrich word meaning by pointing out that *pet* is not only the *name* of something, but also it can tell us what we *do* to the *pet—pet it*.

*Step 4* (Refer to pages 179.)

*The teacher* should ask a child to read, "the first word," "the next word," or "the first two words," "the first column of words," "the last column of words," etc.

*An individual child* should read as directed.

*The group* should repeat *after each word is spoken*—unless the word is read incorrectly, whereupon they remain silent until a correction is made.

*The same procedure should be continued* until the teacher is sure that sufficient practice was provided in the first three steps, so that recall is reasonably "fixed."

D.   READING FROM THE BOOK (Refer to pages 185 and 186 through 198.)

Each child should have his own book and not be expected to share the same copy with another. Otherwise, perception becomes distorted and attention is distracted.

An example of one way to develop thoughtful reading, eye span and recall of the words practiced during the period of Preparation is given below.

*Procedure—to help develop phrase-concept*

After the children have found the right page, the name of the story, and there has been brief discussion of the story in general, they should be asked to place the side of their hands under the first line. (Refer to page 186.)

*The teacher* should say,

"The first word names the person who said something."—"Yes, *Bobby*. It says *Bobby said*." "Look at the next *one* word. It tells us to *do* something. What?"

*A child's* answer should be,

see.

*The teacher*,

"Yes—*see*. What do the other words tell us to see?"

*A child,*

the pony.

*The teacher,*

"Read the whole sentence, and pause a little after you read *Bobby said* to keep that separated from the words that he used when he talked.

*A child,*

Bobby said ⏜   see the pony ⏜.

Word-by-word reading should not be accepted, even if the teacher must demonstrate how the child should speak in the natural rhythm of speech, and have the child repeat.

*The teacher,*

"In the next sentence, find the *one word* that tells what kind of a pony it is."

*A child,*

little.

Accept only the one word *little* as the answer because it is all that answers the question asked by the teacher. The whole sentence should not be read. The child should be alerted to use his ears before performing; otherwise, the teacher should remind him that he did not answer the question as it was asked.

*The teacher,*

"Now read the whole sentence. Tell yourself to pause just a little after the first word and then put the last three words together. That last phrase will tell *what*."

*A child,*

See ⏜   the little pony ⏜.

*The teacher* should ask an individual child to

"Read both sentences to us," and

*a child* should have a turn to do so.

*The teacher,*

"In the next paragraph you will see that a new word we already have practiced is at the end of the sentence. Put your finger under it (and check to see that fingers are correctly placed). What is it?"—"Yes, *toy*."—"Everybody read the whole sentence to yourselves by putting the first two words together, and then pausing a little to let your eyes look ahead to see the last three words."

Allow a little time for all to follow the direction before calling upon someone to read aloud.

*A child,*

⌒        ⌒
*The pony   is a toy.*

To give children experience in verbalizing,

*the teacher* should ask a child to *tell in his own words* what Bobby said about the pony.

*The child* called upon should answer in a sentence—and be given help in sentence construction, if necessary. He might say,

"*It said the pony is a toy,*" or "*It is a toy,*" or "*Bobby said that the pony is a toy,*" etc.

*The teacher,*

"Read the next sentence to yourselves to find out what else he said about the pony. Be sure to stop for just a second after you read the first two words so your eyes can look ahead to see the next words."

*A child*, reading aloud,

⌒        ⌒
*The pony   is my toy.*

*The teacher,*

"Read the last sentence. What does Bobby want you to do? Tell us in your own words."

Because *the teacher's* direction tells the child to verbalize,

*the child*, should answer in his own words, which might be:

*"Bobby wants us to see his toy,"* or *"He wants us to look at it,"* etc.

*The teacher* should ask the same child to read the whole paragraph, and

*the child* should do so.

*Another child* should be asked to read the whole page before going on to the next page.

After *the group* has moved to the next page,

*the teacher* should say,

"There are no new words on this page. Read the first sentence to yourselves. Be sure to let your eyes rest in the right places."

*A child,*

*My pony͡    is little͡    said Bobby,* or

*My pony is͡    little͡    said Bobby.*

If a child reads, *My pony͡    is little said,* ask the child if Bobby would "talk like this" and demonstrate, by saying, *My pony is little said,* enabling him to hear and see for himself how meaning can be lost by incorrect phrasing.

*The teacher,*

"Read the whole paragraph to yourselves. Pause in the right places for the phrases to be understood when you read aloud to us."

*Different* children should be given turns to read aloud after a brief study period.

If there is time, two or three children should read the two pages, each one reading a paragraph or a page.

In the next lesson, the story should be completed.

**EXAMPLE 1 OF A TWO-DAY DAILY LESSON PLAN    PRE-PRIMER LEVEL**

SECOND DAY

VISUAL APPROACH

A.    ALPHABET CARDS

Spend no more than 3 to 4 minutes of drill at the most.

Use the same letters as those used in the previous lesson. If a letter, such as, *p* has been introduced in the meantime, during the LEARNING TO WRITE and AUDITORY APPROACH periods, it should be included.

B.    UNLOCKING WORDS

With the following words, use the procedure for AUDITORY-visual-kinesthetic association *explained on page 159:*

| | |
|---|---|
| see | my |
| toy | little |
| said | pony |
| pet | Bobby |

If a word whose initial letter has not been taught, (such as *very*) is included in a list, the teacher should not name it. It would be there only for the sake of discrimination.

READING

The reading material appears on page 199-200.

C.    PREPARATION FOR READING—For Phrase Recognition
(Refer to page 175.)

*Phrase list*—structured steps explained on pages 180 through page 184. The new words are underlined.

| | |
|---|---|
| My *pony* | pony |
| *with* my toy | with |
| I *can* play | can |
| can *not* play | not |
| with *my* pony | my |
| not a *pet* | pet |

Placing the new words at the right of the phrases need not be done always. It affords extra practice and association, especially for the group with a greater degree of disability.

*The teacher* should follow the same four steps used to develop single word recognition.

*Step 1* (Refer to pages 180-181.)–*Visual-Auditory-Kinesthetic*

*The teacher* should read each phrase in the natural rhythm of speech–not word-by-word.

*The group of children* should repeat each phrase *after* it has been read–not with the teacher.

*An individual child*, who may need extra help in speaking, should be given opportunity to repeat and to receive help where needed.

*Step 2* (Refer to pages 181-182.)–*Auditory-Visual-Kinesthetic*

*The teacher* should read any one of the phrases–*but should not point to it.*

*A child* should find, and place the pointer under the correct phrase, and read in a natural rhythm for all to hear, and for him to *feel* the words in his own speech organs.

*The group* should repeat, unless an error in reading is made, such as, failures to add final *s* or a suffix.

*The teacher* should follow the same procedure, skipping around the column of phrases so the children must look from phrase to phrase in order to find the right one.

*Step 3* (Refer to pages 182-183-184.) *Concept-Auditory-Visual-Kinesthetic*

*The teacher* should give the meaning of a phrase.

*A child* should find, place the pointer under the phrase, and read.

*The group* should repeat.

As an example, *the teacher* might ask *a child* to find a phrase that tells:

| | |
|---|---|
| — what you can *do*— | *I can play* |
| — that something belongs to you,— | *my pony* |
| — what someone *can not do*, | *can not play* |
| — what his pony is, | *not a pet* |
| — what you play with, | *with my toy* |
| | or |
| | *with my pony* |

207

The teacher might ask the same child to find another phrase that means the same or, in the first questioning, might have asked the child to read two phrases that had somewhat the same meaning. *The group* should repeat after each phrase is read.

*Step 4* (Refer to pages 184-.)—*Visual-Auditory-Kinesthetic*

*Individual children* should have turns to read one or two phrases, and

*the group* should repeat after each phrase is read—or remain silent if it is read incorrectly.

Children should be able to recognize and read the phrases independently if enough time was spent with the first three steps.

As a last check, *the teacher* should ask *a child* to read the new words shown at the right of the column of phrases.

If a child should hesitate on any one of the words, encourage him to find it within the phrase, for its association with phrase concept, if possible, to assist recall. Also, the teacher might give the meaning of the word to help link an association to trigger recall.

D.   READING FROM THE BOOK (Refer to page 185 and to pages 186-199.)

*Procedure*—to help develop rhythm, eye span, and concept-phrase reading.

As a review of the previous day's lesson, and before continuing with the new page,

*the teacher* should ask a child to tell (for verbalizing thought) what *two* things Bobby told about the pony.

*A child*, speaking in a sentence, should say that the pony was a *toy* and it was *little*.

Then, to continue with the reading, *the teacher* should say,

"Put your hand under the first line, and study it to prepare yourself to read the phrases correctly."

*A child,*

My pony‿   is a toy‿   said Bobby, or

My pony is‿   a toy‿   said Bobby.

If a child reads word-by-word—*my   pony*—the teacher should tap the rhythm on the child's shoulder so it can be felt—*my pony*.

Children should be encouraged to swing their arms to feel the rhythm, as explained in Step 1 on pages 180 and 181.

The teacher never should despair if some children are slow to feel the rhythm in association with phrase concept. This weakness appears frequently in children with auditory-kinesthetic disability. With day by day help, the desired change occurs, usually beginning in less than ten days. They do not become bored or discouraged because the personal attention helps them learn. The teacher's task is to prevent a feeling of failure, and to help develop patterns of performance as well as patterns for thought in these first year SLD beginners. The reward comes with the look on a child's face when cognition occurs, and a new kind of independent self-direction is gained—the best kind of motivation.

*The teacher,*

"What words in that first sentence are used to remind us of the one who is talking?"—"Yes, *said Bobby*. We *cannot hear* him therefore the book has to *tell* us."

"In the next sentence, put the first three words together and then the last three words. They will go together like this," and the rhythm should be tapped out for its auditory perception by children in the group.

*A child,*

I can play    with my pony.

*The teacher,*

"In the third sentence, the first two words tell what Bobby says he does."

*A child,*

I play.

*The teacher,*

"With what?"

*The child,*

with my toy pony.

*The teacher,*

"Read the whole sentence in good phrasing."

*The child,*

$\overset{\frown}{I\ play}$   $\overset{\frown}{with\ my\ toy\ pony}.$

*On the last page,*

   *the teacher* should give the direction,

   "Now you study this last page by yourselves. Read the first sentence to yourselves and when you are ready to read it aloud in good phrasing, let me know."

*A child* should read, or even reread where necessary.

   *Sometimes only one sentence might need to be reread for self-improvement of phrase concept and rhythm. The children should be led into the understanding that these reading lessons provide the only time they will receive teacher-help that will enable them to read independently and with comprehension of what is being read.*

*The teacher* should continue in the same way, sentence-by-sentence until the page is completed.

When the whole story is completed, the teacher should ask a few questions for summarization, thought, and verbalization, regardless of how simple the story.

*The teacher,*

   "I will ask some *thinking* questions for you to answer."

*Examples* of questions and possible answers to encourage children's thought:

   — "Who did all the talking in this story?"—
"Yes, Bobby."

   — "To whom might he have been talking?"—
(to himself; to a friend; to us; etc.)

   — "Do Bobby and his pony *play together* or does
Bobby *play with* his pony?"—
"That's right, *he* plays *with* his pony."

   — "Why can they not play together?"—
"Of course, the pony is just a toy."

— "Who had to do all the *thinking* for this kind
of play?"—
"That's right, *Bobby did*, and you know why."

If there is time, have the story reread orally for fluency and because the children should
have a better comprehension of what they are reading when it is reread.

After this group of children returns to their own seats to carry out assigned work* , the
teacher should help another group that reads at either a lower or more advanced level.

## E.    INDEPENDENT READING

As soon as the assigned work has been completed, the children should be encouraged to
read independently from phonetic readers that contain words formed with consonants and
vowels they have learned how to use in unlocking words.**

---

*Ibid.
**Barbara Makar, *Primary Phonics Storybooks* 1-10; Anna Gillingham, *Little Stories;* Bessie Stillman,
*The Teacup Whale*; Mary Helen Burnett, *First Phonics*. All these books are available through Educators
Publishing Service, Inc., Cambridge, Mass.

**EXAMPLE 2 OF A TWO-DAY LESSON PLAN    PRIMER LEVEL**

FIRST DAY

VISUAL APPROACH

A.   ALPHABET CARDS

Assuming that most of the consonants and the vowels *a* and *i*, and the consonant digraphs *ck* and *sh* have been learned during the LEARNING TO WRITE and AUDITORY APPROACH periods, the cards might include:

b   c   d   f   g   h   j   k   l   m   n   s   t   p   r   w
a   i       ck   sh

(Refer to pages 154 through 156 for procedures and a variation in practice.)

B.   UNLOCKING—for discrimination of short *a* and short *i*, a *word list* such as the one shown below might be used. (Refer to pages 166 through 170.)

| glad | ran | back | fish | cab |
|------|-----|------|------|-----|
| fast | sad | lift | wish | gift |
| can | him | jig | shack | task |
| will | did | pick | hash | wilt |
| big | and | wag | dish | win |

*The teacher* should tell the children that the first two columns contain words that will appear in the story to be read. If they fail to recognize them when reading, they will be able to work them out for themselves.

*Each child* in the group should have one or two turns to:

1) find and name the vowel,
2) name the key word,
3) give the short vowel sound,
4) pronounce the word.

READING

The reading material might be as follows:

BOBBY WANTS A PET

*Page 1*                          Bobby and mother and daddy came to
                                 their new home.

212

How glad they were!
They got out of their car and
they stood and looked.

Mother looked at the white house.
Daddy looked at the big yard.
Bobby looked at the big tree and he
saw something in one tree.

*Page 2*
Something went fast.
It went up in the tree.
Then it went down in the tree.
It stopped and looked at Bobby.

"Look, Mother. Look, Daddy,"
cried Bobby.
"Do you see what I see?
See that little squirrel.
That squirrel can be my pet and
we can play together.
I will get him now."
Away he ran very fast.

*Page 3*
Mother cried, "Stop, Bobby.
The little squirrel does not know
you yet.
He is not a pet squirrel."
But Bobby did not stop.

Bobby cried, "I want him. I like
him and he is not a toy.
I want this squirrel for my pet.
We can play together every day."

Bobby ran to the tree and called
to the squirrel.
"Come down to me, Squirrel,"
he cried.
But the squirrel did not come
down.

*Page 4*
"Bobby, you will frighten the
little squirrel," called Daddy.
"He will not come down to you yet."
Bobby did not stop.

Bobby began to go up the tree.
The squirrel went up, too.
Bobby went up and up.
The squirrel went up and up, and up
and up and up.
Bobby had to stop.

*Page 5*

Bobby came down from the tree.
He looked very sad, and he said,
"That squirrel will not come down.
We can not play together."

Daddy said, "You went too fast,
Bobby.
Let us think why you can not play
together.
Let us think what you can do.
By and by that squirrel may want to
play with you."

C.    PREPARATION—For Phrase Recognition
(Refer to page 175.)

*Phrase List.* (Refer to pages 180 through 184.)

their new home
How glad
stood and looked
at the yard
something went fast
that little squirrel
does not know you yet
together every day

*Step 1*

Follow the usual procedure explained on pages 180-181.

*The teacher* should point out that:

— in the first phrase, the word *their* shows ownership of more than one.

— the phrase *stood and looked* is a past time phrase, and attention should be directed
to *how many* things someone did.—(two)

— in the phrase *that little squirrel*, one word indicates which particular squirrel.—(that)

— the word *yet* in the last phrase is a "time" word meaning *up to now*.

Some SLD children have difficulty with "time" orientation so they need help with such words as *yet, before, now*, etc., in association with temporal or time concept.

*Step 2*

The same procedure explained on pages 181-182 should be followed.

*Step 3* The same procedure explained on pages 182-183-184 should be followed.

Some suggestions are given below:

"Find the phrase that: (Phrases on previous page)

— tells *how* something moved." (5th phrase)
— tells at *what* they might have looked." (any one of the
1st, 4th or 6th phrases or all of them)
— tells *what* someone does not know." (7th phrase)
— tells *when*." (8th phrase)
— *gives an idea* of happiness or good feeling.
(2nd phrase)

*Step 4*

The same procedure explained on pages 184 should be followed.

D.   READING FROM THE BOOK (Refer to pages 185 through 198, and to pages 202 through 205 and 208 through 211.)

How much of the reading lesson can be covered—two or three pages—depends on the time allowed, the ability of the group, and the severity of the disabilities.

When children following along in this continuum of instruction have reached primer level in reading achievement, it can be assumed that they are gaining reasonable phrase cognition. Thus the teacher should be able to spend less time in directing eye span for the phrasing and understanding of each sentence. Children should be directed to read one or two sentences, or even a short paragraph to themselves, enabling them to have opportunity to phrase correctly before being given turns to read aloud.

The teacher should not hesitate to have a child reread if phrasing is incorrect, the rhythm lost, or meaning distorted or misunderstood.

**The teacher's obligation is to teach and guide in the development of SLD children's patterning for reading and conceptualizing what is read. It is not enough that pages be assigned for silent reading: otherwise, specific individual needs are overlooked or unrecognized. Oral reading should be a vital part of each day's lesson.**

Below are some suggestions for thoughtful recall of a story introduced in a previous pre-primer lesson.

*The teacher*,

"Do you remember, a long time ago, we read how Bobby had a toy pony but he and the toy could not play together for a special reason. Why could they not *play with each other—together?*" Have children verbalize their recall of the reason.

"The name of this story lets you know what he wants and as we read it we will find out something else about playing together—*with each other.*" (*Both must participate in a common purpose,* even if both can think and play.) (Refer to pages 212 through 214.)

*The teacher*,

"Read the first three lines to yourselves to find out why everyone was glad."

*A child* should be given a turn to read the lines.

*The teacher*,

"Now tell us in your own words, not the book's words."

*A child* should verbalize in his words.

*The teacher*,

"Study the next two lines which make the next sentence, and then read just the part that tells what all of them did first."

*A child* should read aloud,

 *got out  of their car*

*The teacher*,

"Now read what else all of them did."

*A child,*

*stood and looked*

*The teacher* should ask *a child* to read the whole paragraph and then ask that someone *verbalize what the whole family did together.*

*The teacher,*

"Study the next paragraph to yourselves, and find out what they did not do together. You will notice that each one was thinking about something different."

*Individual children* should read paragraphs orally, should verbalize and, having turns, reread orally the pages studied.

The same procedure should be followed with each page for as long as the period allows. The unfinished portions should be continued in the succeeding lesson.

*When children return to their seats* they should be encouraged to reread to themselves what was studied, and to continue to read on, if desired and there is ability to do so.

**EXAMPLE 2 OF A TWO-DAY LESSON PLAN    PRIMER LEVEL**

SECOND DAY

VISUAL APPROACH

A.    ALPHABET CARDS

About five minutes should be allowed for review of all the letters and consonant digraphs that have been taught. If *ch* had been introduced during previous LEARNING TO WRITE and AUDITORY APPROACH periods, it should be included in this practice for visual recall and auditory-kinesthetic association. (Refer to pages 154 through 156.)

If the Alphabet Cards have been used for practice with the entire class at an earlier period, they should be omitted at the beginning of the reading lessons with each group. If not, they should be given a brief review at the beginning of each group lesson. In the course of time, different groups, reading at different levels, should have more or less cards, depending upon the achievement of each group.

B.    UNLOCKING—For practice in unlocking only such words as contain short vowels that have been taught.

As many words using *ch* as possible should be presented for practice in unlocking.*

| | | | | |
|---|---|---|---|---|
| chip | chick | cast | wag | ranch |
| chap | rich | tack | wig | pinch |
| chill | chaff | tick | rim | chant |
| champ | chad | gasp | wish | inch |
| lamp | chimp | task | gilt | chin |

Do not use *tch* until it has been taught.

*The teacher* should follow the same procedure already explained on page 212. As each child has his turn he should underline the vowel with chalk as it is named.

This same kind of drill can be given without underlining the vowel, but it sometimes is advisable to do so when introducing consonant digraphs. It helps children perceive the *ch* as a whole while moving from left to right to find the vowel that "opens the throat," or when looking on beyond the vowel, to perceive the final symbol-sound.

*Slingerland, *Phonetic Word Lists,* page 10 and *Teacher's Word Lists,* page 16.

218

C.   PREPARATION FOR WORD RECOGNITION—From the reading material shown on pages 212-213, 214

*Word List*—to be placed on the blackboard.

|   |   |
|---|---|
| know | squirrel |
| together | what |
| their | frighten |
| stopped | stood |

*The teacher* should follow the same *four steps* explained on pages 176 through 184.

After, *not before*, the words have been learned, a game to help motivate and to fix vocabulary, such as the one suggested below, can be played.

*The Game*—The child having a "turn" should stand behind the first of the seated children of the group. The teacher should point to one of the words. Whichever of the two children reads the word first may be the one to have the next turn to stand and try to read the word before the seated child. For as long as the *standing child* is the winner he may move from child to child. If a *seated child* wins, he may have the "turn" and the other child takes his seat.

If a child is able to win each time as he moves from child to child in the whole group, he is called a "winner," and other children are given turns.

Every child must include final *s's* and *suffixes* to be a "winner."

Playing such a game should not be extended beyond a time that does not interfere with the actual reading from the book, under teacher guidance.

D.   READING FROM THE BOOK

*The teacher* should have a child or two verbalize a brief summary of what was read in the previous lesson. Help should be given with sentence construction, if needed, by suggesting that the child speak first of *what he is to talk about* and then to say *something about it*.

*The children* should be directed to read silently a sentence or two or a "paragraph" so that phrasing will be correct when they read aloud.

Sometimes *the teacher* should ask a child to read (as on page 3 of 213) *the sentence* that "tells why Mother wanted Bobby to stop." *(The little squirrel does not know you yet)*, or *the phrase* that "tells what Bobby thought he and the squirrel could do" *(play together every day)*.

When the story is completed, a summary of the main points should be made through discussion and questioning. In this particular story the reason why Bobby and the squirrel could not play together as he had hoped should be elicited—(*playing together* requires mutual purpose, even when children play).

The entire story should be reread to give turns to all for oral reading.

SLD children do not become bored when learning *how to be able* to read and to understand what they are reading.

**EXAMPLE 3 OF A DAILY LESSON PLAN    FIRST GRADE LEVEL**

VISUAL APPROACH

A.   ALPHABET CARDS

When the pack of cards is to be used with *the entire class*, from 5-7, and, possibly, 10 minutes should be allowed. If a card known only by the children in a more advanced reading group is exposed, one of the children in that group should be called upon. The class should repeat. Children in more slowly advancing groups should be called upon to tell about the exposed letters they have been taught, and the whole class should repeat after each individual performance.

When this drill is not to be used with the entire class, it should be used as an introduction to *each group's* reading lesson with the teacher. Each group's pack should be expected to be different because levels of achievement will not be the same.

> As groups advance, the children are able to learn consonants, vowel digraphs, vowel-consonant-e, diphthongs, letter combinations, and other phonograms much faster for reading than for spelling.*

B.   UNLOCKING

*A Word List for Review*—containing learned consonants, short vowels, digraphs and suffixes in various letter arrangements.

> Children should have had experience with suffixes by the time they reach this point in their reading achievement. (Refer to AUDITORY APPROACH, pages 108-113 and 133—, etc.)

The list of words should be written in manuscript.

| | | | |
|---|---|---|---|
| blimp | tramped | crust | which |
| blast | blocks | whack | mashing |
| blasting | trucking | spun | trust |
| slumped | chanted | wilt | trusting |
| lunch | chug | shift | chops |

*Examples of unlocking procedures*

> *Children* should say when looking at:

> blimp—i, /ĭ/, *blimp*
> tramped—a, /ă/, *tramp, tramped*

*Slingerland, *Teacher's Word Lists*.

221

Eventually the children are able to include the suffixes at the moment the root word is perceived and recognized, but *in this practice* the children should be told that they are to name the root word first, and then repeat the root word with its suffix. Then their "thought pattern" will become *automatic*, and they will be able to help themselves when reading by themselves.

trusting—u, /ŭ/, *trust, trusting*

chops—o, /ŏ/, *chop, chops*

*The teacher* should remind the children that:

  — all the letters up to the vowel should be
      blended together.

  — all the letters that follow the vowel in
      (one-syllable) words, or follow the vowel up
      to the suffix, should be blended together.

  — in working out words, the suffixes should be
      added after the root word is recognized or
      unlocked.

READING

## C.   PREPARATION FOR READING

Phrases from the reading material for the day's lesson should be placed on the blackboard in manuscript.

The four steps, explained on page 175 and on pages 180 through 184 for Visual-Auditory-Kinesthetic association to strengthen perception, recall, concept, and eye span should be followed, always emphasizing Step 2.

## D.   READING FROM THE BOOK

With the first page or several paragraphs *the teacher* should guide *individual children's* reading through several sentences or a paragraph. Then the reading should be "studied aloud" until the period with this particular group is concluded. (Refer to page 192.) Unfinished pages should be continued in the next day's lesson. The group should return to their seats to:

1  complete assigned work,*
2  reread the story just studied,
3  read independently.**

*The teacher* should help another group that will be reading at another level, and, probably, from different material which requires entirely different lesson planning.

The reading periods are not "free time," but instead, they are times to show consideration for other groups while they are being given their special instruction by the teacher. The teacher should devote her attention to the group at hand and not to giving individual instruction to children outside the reading group working with her.

E.   INDEPENDENT READING

Each group should reread the story or stories on which they already have been given guidance, or they should read from phonetic and library books easily available for individual choice.**

*O'Neal and Zylstra, *Independent Creative Ideas*.

**Phonetic books such as those listed in the footnote on page 211, and library books with simple vocabulary that is below the instructional level, allowing for a range in the selection to be made by individual children.

**EXAMPLE 4 OF A DAILY LESSON PLAN WITH TWO DIFFERENT GROUPS IN THE SAME CLASS** FIRST GRADE LEVEL—Less Advanced Group and More Advanced Group

THE LESS ADVANCED GROUP

VISUAL APPROACH

A.   ALPHABET CARDS

*Introducing tch*

*The teacher* should:

1  show the *tch* Alphabet Card,
2  name the letters as they are formed with a free arm swing,
3  name the key word *catch*,
4  give the sound /ch/. (Refer to page 52.)

It should be pointed out to the children that:

1  *ch* and *tch* have exactly the same sound,
2  the three letters should be seen as *one unit* because they stay together to make *one sound*,
3  *tch* will *never* appear at the beginning of a word or syllable *(hatch et)*.

*Individual children* should be given turns to "tell about" *tch* in the usual way:

1  *t c h* , forming each letter as it is named,
2  *catch*,
3  /ch/.

Sometimes a single letter or a letter unit (trigraph) such as *tch* can be introduced to the entire class—all the groups at one time—or just to the one group ready to learn. If introduced to all, its use in unlocking words should be given in B—UNLOCKING, to the entire class also.

The *tch* Alphabet Card should be added to the Alphabet Card pack for future practice. (Refer to pages 53 through page 55.)

When used in the AUDITORY APPROACH, A—Alphabet Card practice, the teacher should name the key word to help the children determine whether to spell the sound with *ch* or *tch*. For example:

"What says /ch/ as in *catch*? or

"What says /ch/ as in *chair*?"

Not until ambiguous spelling is introduced, in the 2nd and 3rd year of this instructional continuum, should the child be expected to tell all of the ways of spelling a given sound, such as /ch/, or /oi/, or /ā/, etc.* It is much more difficult for SLD children to recall *which way* to spell a given sound, when there are several ways, than for them to associate the correct sound with an exposed visual symbol.

B.   UNLOCKING

*Each child* should have a turn, or turns, to unlock such words—written in manuscript—as appear below.

| patch | botch | thatch | ditch | switching |
| latch | Dutch | witch | notch | switched |
| hutch | hitch | batch | match | matches |
| stitch | pitch | hatch | clutch | patched |

As an example with the word *patch*, a child should say,

"*A*, /ă/, *patch*,"

and with the word *switching*,

"*I*, /ĭ/, switch, *switching*."

For READING refer to page 228.

*Slingerland, *Teacher's Word Lists,* page 1.

**EXAMPLE 4 OF A DAILY LESSON PLAN WITH THE MORE ADVANCED GROUP — FIRST GRADE LEVEL**

VISUAL APPROACH

*Combining A—Alphabet Cards and B—Unlocking to Introduce vowel-consonant-e (silent-e) for READING\**

When Specific Language Disability children with developmental readiness due to chronological ages, general maturity, background, and eagerness to learn (unless previous experiences have brought about strong emotional blockages) are introduced to this multi-sensory approach *in their second year* of school, they often progress more rapidly than beginners. However, many SLD beginners have the maturity and general developmental background to make commendable progress when this technique is used as a "preventive" measure to preclude possible failure or inadequate performance. Their ability to learn to read often outstrips their ability to spell and to do written work. *Therefore, what is learned for reading need not necessarily be a parallel learning for spelling at this time.*

As an example for teaching *vowel-consonant-e,*

the teacher should write a word, such as *pan*, on the blackboard and say,

"If I see this word I can work it out by saying—*a*, (*apple*), /ă/, *pan*—but by adding this one little *e* to *pan* it looks like this now—*pane*. It says something entirely different, too. This *e* is called a *silent-e* because it makes no sound in a word like this. It is there just to make this first vowel *a* say its own name—/ā/. The word is worked out like this: *a-consonant-e*, /ā/, *pane*."

*The teacher* should point to the word, and to each letter about which she is speaking, so that the children can see and hear to assist in building this association.

The *a-e Alphabet Card* should be exposed and the children told that the *key word* is *safe*. It should be written on the blackboard for all to see. They should be told that the little line between the *a* and the *e* stands for whatever consonant happens to be needed in a particular word. Demonstrate with the key word as shown below:

safe

a-e

| a-e |
| --- |

(Refer to the picture of the Phonogram Chart shown on page 30.)

---

\*Ibid., pages 37 and 38.

*Individual children* should "tell about" the *a-e* Alphabet Card in the usual way, and by forming the little line between the *a* and the *e* when saying *consonant a-consonant-e, safe,* /ā/.

The *Alphabet Card* should be included in the Card Pack.

When used in VISUAL APPROACH practice, the card should be exposed for the child to tell about. (Refer to pages 52-53.)

When used in AUDITORY APPROACH practice, the teacher should ask, "What says /ā/ as in *safe?*" and the child should answer in the usual way. (Refer to pages 53-54.)

*Teacher judgment* must determine when the group is ready to learn how this same *silent-e* will change the sounds of other vowels to their *name sounds, long sounds.* SLD children usually are unable to abstract readily until the task of learning *a-e words* becomes reasonably automatic. When this has been accomplished, *i-e, u-e,* etc., should be introduced, and the children usually abstract without difficulty. The key to successful performance in abstracting is to learn well the first task—unlocking a-e words.

When *the children* have been given turns to tell about the exposed card, and to recall *a-e* when it appears among other exposed cards during practice with the Pack, a word list for *B—Unlocking* should be presented.

*A-e Word List*\*—written in manuscript:

| | | | |
|------|-------|-------|-------|
| lame | slave | game | quake |
| lake | bake | wade | plane |
| raze | flare | haze | skate |
| babe | tape | shave | shake |
| pale | tame | chase | cane |

*Each child* should have a turn, or turns, to unlock a word in the following way:

shave — *a-consonant-e*, using a free arm swing,
(safe), /ā/, *shave*

quake — *a-consonat-e*, using free arm swing,
(safe), /ā/, *quake*

\*Ibid., page 38.
and
Slingerland, *Phonetic Word Lists,* page 33.

If a child is more secure in his recall by naming the key word, he should *be allowed* to do so.

If a child hesitates or makes mistakes in his recall, he should *be required* to name the key word until recall is securely fixed and response is automatic.

In succeeding lessons, copies of *Phonetic Word Lists for Children's Use** can be placed in each child's hands to enable each to read the first two columns of *a-e words* from the printed page instead of the blackboard. *A-c-e* and *a-g-e* words should be avoided until soft *c* and *g* have been taught.

FIRST GRADE LEVEL—Advanced Group and less Advanced Group

## READING

### C.   PREPARATION

Practice with phrases or words for visual-auditory-kinesthetic association should be taken from whatever reading material is being used with each individual group.

One group may be well along in first grade level material; another group may be beginning first grade level; a third group may be progressing more slowly at primer level.

This necessitates teacher planning suitable for each individual group's achievement ability, *but the basic approach in using the Four Steps should be the same.*. (Refer to pages 175 through 184.)

### D.   READING FROM THE BOOK

Regardless of how well each group may be advancing, part of the reading period should be devoted to *structuring*, sometimes emphasizing phrasing, understanding of punctuation marks, conceptualizing, or unlocking, etc. (Refer to pages 185-199; 202-206; 208 through 211; 215-218.)

*Structuring* on some occasions while studying together under teacher guidance should emphasize one or more means of attacking unfamiliar or unrecognized words on the pages of the reading material.

*A Few Suggestions*

1. When a child hesitates on a phonetic word (phonetic to the child), the teacher should have the child work out the word aloud by using the same technique already learned during *B—Unlocking* periods. (Refer to page 162.) Realization that a word among other words on the page is phonetic and can be worked out may be missed in a figure-background confusion. To work out a list of words on the blackboard under a controlled situation does serve as an initial step to learning how to unlock, *but the carry-over into actual use in reading from a page requires another kind of structured guidance and no pressure whatsoever for speed.*

*Ibid, page 33.

228

2. With a phonetic word, such as *planter*, the child should be told to cover the suffix *er* with his thumb, to work out the root word *(plant)*, and then to read it with the suffix added.

3. With a non-phonetic word, such as *washing*, whose root word has been learned in previous lessons, the child should be told to cover the suffix with his thumb—a device that often triggers immediate perception and recall. If not, the teacher should associate the meaning with the word by saying, "It means what we do to clean our hands," and by reminding the child to "look at the very first letter (w) and shape your lips into its formation to feel how the word begins,"—a kinesthetic reinforcement. If the child still does not recognize the word, it should be named by the teacher for the child to repeat, including the suffix.

4. With a phonetic word whose suffix has not been taught, such as *wishful*, the child should be told to cover *f u l* , the suffix, and to read (or work out) the root word, and then to add the suffix which should be named for the child by the teacher.

5. With a known non-phonetic word whose suffix has not been taught, such as *laughable*, the child should be told to cover the suffix *a b l e* and to read the root word. The suffix should be pronounced /a ble'/ for the child who, in turn, usually is able then to read the whole word.

6. With a word containing two consonants in the medial position, such as *trimmed*, the child should be taught to divide the word between the two consonants—by covering, with his finger, all the letters after the first *m*—enabling him to perceive the root word, and then to read it with its suffix.

The teacher should assist children to "abstract" with root word-suffix reading by encouraging them to look from the beginning of a word to its ending, and, if a suffix is seen, to disregard ("pay no attention to") it for the moment or until the root word is recognized. Then "it is easy to add the suffix."

After a reasonable time spent in structuring, and reading aloud during a group's lesson time with the teacher, the children at this level of achievement and maturity are often capable of studying a page or two "on their own" in preparation for the next lesson with the teacher.

*The teacher* should be freed by this to give help to one of the other individuals or groups.

*The teacher* should be free to give help to one of the other groups while these children work "on their own".

E.　INDEPENDENT READING

Phonetic readers or booklets and basic reading material\* below the instructional level, should be placed where children can make their own selections for independent reading. Encouragement should be given for individual preparation of something to read to the class in a *special reading period.*

*Suggestions*

Sometimes two or three children should study together from copies of the same book for preparation and share in the reading of a story to the class during the *special reading* periods.

Sometimes a story should be studied by one or more children. Part of the story should be verbalized and part read aloud during the *special reading* time. Stories frequently are too long to be read aloud in entirety.

\*Phonetic readers such as those listed on page 211, basic readers such as those listed on page 174, and library books.

## SUMMARIZING PROGRESS AND LOOKING AHEAD IN THE VISUAL APPROACH

Each year ends with the first year groups of beginners reading at different levels of achievement. They should be led forward in the second year from the point at which they were able to function when the school year ended. Often, however, they need to begin with some review. Other children may continue to advance during the summer. It is the teacher's responsibility to determine correct group placement early in the school year and to provide a flexibility that permits beneficial transfers from one group to another.*

Specific Language Disability children should not be pressured; neither should they be held back when they begin to gain momentum. *The same organization of a teacher's daily lesson plan* is used with each group within a classroom, regardless of the different reading levels. Also, *the reading techniques are the same.* Consequently, *only the reading material varies* from group to group. This permits the transfer of an individual child to the group that best provides the reading material to serve his instructional level of intake.

In general, *the First Year Continuum in the Visual Approach* of new learnings and experiences should include:

A.  ALPHABET CARDS

— all the consonants and vowels taught in the AUDITORY APPROACH

— all the consonant digraphs taught in the AUDITORY APPROACH

— possibly several vowel digraphs, or diphthongs or phonograms

B.  UNLOCKING**(decoding)

— one-syllable, phonetic, short vowel words containing the vowels taught in the AUDITORY APPROACH

— one-syllable, short vowel phonetic words with suffixes taught in the AUDITORY APPROACH

— possibly, some one-syllable words containing a vowel digraph, or diphthong, or phonogram, such as *ee, ou, oa, ar, er, oo* (from this point on their functional use for reading outstrips that for spelling)

---

*For recording of individual growth, achievement tests are recommended to be administered late in the first year or early in the second year. IT SHOULD BE REMEMBERED THAT IT TAKES FROM TWO TO THREE YEARS FOR SLD CHILDREN TO SHOW AN ACHIEVEMENT COMPARABLE TO NON-DISABILITY BOYS AND GIRLS. They should, however, be judged on the basis of individual progress as measured against their own yearly achievement. Some never achieve more than grade level scores while, for others of high intelligence, this is not enough. They should be kept in an SLD Program for as many years of help as possible or until they can function commensurate with their mental ability.

**Slingerland, *Phonetic Word Lists.*

C.  PREPARATION FOR READING—(4 Steps)

   — word recognition, with concept

   — phrase recognition, with concept

D.  READING FROM A BOOK

   — how to phrase, with concept

   — how to develop eye span—and related to concept

   — functional use of *unlocking* while reading

   — how to study

   — how to verbalize what is read

E.  INDEPENDENT READING

   — material at, or below instructional level

Looking ahead to *the Second Year Continuum*, new learnings and experiences should include:

COPYING—For independent work (a functional need, dependent on LEARNING TO WRITE AS PART OF THE AUDITORY APPROACH)

   — functional use of copying for teacher-assigned tasks

   — functional use for independent needs

A.  ALPHABET CARDS

   — all the consonants—the two sounds of *s, c, g,* etc.,

   — all the vowels—short and long sounds,

   — *y* as a vowel,

   — vowel-consonant-e,

   — more consonant digraphs and, consonant trigraphs—*tch* and *dge,*

— most of the diphthongs, vowel digraphs and phonograms, some of which have more than one sound,

— letter combinations, such as ing, ung, ank, tion, etc.

B.   UNLOCKING* (decoding)

— one-syllable, short vowel words, (all vowels, all consonants, more consonant digraphs and trigraphs),

— one-syllable, short vowel words with suffixes,

— more suffixes, such as *ful, able, less, ness,* etc.,

— vowel-consonant-e (v-e),

— letter combination words containing ong, unk, tion, etc.,

— many words in which diphthongs, vowel digraphs and phonograms give the vowel sound (this as a functional skill will outstrip its use for spelling),

— two-syllable phonetic words and how to divide them into syllables,

— two-syllable phonetic words containing silent-e syllables,** such as fle, ple, zle, etc.,

— introduction of long vowel sounds when the vowel occurs at the end of accented syllables.

## READING

C.   PREPARATION—(4 Steps)

— more difficult word recognition,

— phrase drill with more emphasis on adjective and adverb concept.

D.   READING FROM A BOOK

— continuing to phrase, with concept,

— recognizing broken phrases when part is on one line and part on the next line,

— eye span related to word recognition and concept.

*Slingerland, *Phonetic Word Lists,*
**Ibid, page 42 and *Teacher's Word Lists,* page 47.

– continued functional use of *unlocking* while reading from a page,

–continued concept building through understanding of paragraphs and conversation of the story characters as conveyors of meaning to be imparted by the author.

– how to verbalize what is read or the answers to questions,

– how to study independently,

–how to use teacher-child study of long stories or social studies, science, number or health books, etc.

E.   INDEPENDENT READING

– material at, or below instructional level for pleasure,

– to obtain information.

Suggested Bibliography for
Specific Language Disability Teachers

1. Bakwin, Harry (D.D.), editor, *The Pediatric Clinics of North America*, Vol. 15, No. 3, August, 1968. W.B. Saunders, Co., Philadelphia.

2. Bannatyne, Alex. D., "A Suggested Classification of the Causes of Dyslexia." *Word Blind Bulletin*, Vol. 1, No. 5, Spring, 1966.

3. _____"Diagnostic and Remedial Techniques for Use with Dyslexic Children." *Word Blind Bulletin*, Vol. 1, Nos. 6 and 7, Winter, 1966.

4. _____"The Transfer from Modality Perceptual to Modality Conceptual." A paper read at the International Reading Association Annual Convention, Seattle, Washington, May, 1967.

5. _____"Matching Remedial Methods with Specific Deficits." International Convocation on Children and Young Adults With Learning Disabilities, 1967.

6. _____"Verbal and Spatial Abilities, and Reading." Paper presented at the First International Reading Association Congress, August, 1966, Paris, France.

7. Bender, Lauretta, "Specific Reading Disability as a Maturational Lag." *The Bulletin of the Orton Society*, Vol. 7, 1957.

8. Boder, Elena, "A Neuropediatric Approach to the Diagnosis and Management of School Behavioral and Learning Disorders." LEARNING DISORDERS Vol. II, edited by J. Hellmuth, Seattle, Special Child Publications, 1966.

9. Bryant, N. Dale, "Learning Disabilities in Reading." A pre-publication draft, Pre-publication Draft Department of Pediatrics, Albany, Albany Medical College.

10. _____"Some Principles of Remedial Instruction for Dyslexia." Pre-Publication Draft, Albany, Albany Medical College.

11. _____"Characteristics of Dyslexia and Their Remedial Implication." *Exceptional Children*, Vol. 31, No. 4, December, 1965.

12. Bryant, N. Dale and Paul Patterson, "Reading Disability: Part of a Syndrome of Neurological Dysfunctioning." Presented at International Reading Association, 1962.

13. Chall, Jeanne, LEARNING TO READ; THE GREAT DEBATE. New York, McGraw-Hill, 1967.

14. Childs, Sally B., "Sound Reading." New Frontiers in Reading Proceedings, International Reading Association, 1960 (an Orton Society reprint).

15. Childs, Sally B. and Ralph deS. Childs, SOUND SPELLING. Cambridge, Mass., Educators Publishing Service, Inc., 1968.

16. Clemmens, Raymond L., "Obscure Causes of School Failure—A Pediatric Point of View." The Orton Society, Monograph 1, 1965 (an Orton Society reprint).

17. Cole, Edwin M. and Louise Walker, "Familial Patterns of Expression of Specific Reading Disability in a Population Sample." *The Bulletin of the Orton Society*, Vol. XV, 1965 (an Orton Society reprint).

18. Cole, Edwin M., "Specific Reading Disability." *The American Journal of Ophthalmology*, 34 (1949).

19. Critchley, Macdonald, DEVELOPMENTAL DYSLEXIA. Springfield, Charles Thomas, 1964.
20. Crosby, N.N. and Robert A. Liston, THE WAYSIDERS: *An Approach to Reading and the Dyslexic Child*. New York, Delacorte Press, 1968.
21. deHirsch, Katrina, Jeannette Jansky and William Langford, PREDICTING READING FAILURE. New York, Harper and Row, 1967.
22. deHirsch, Katrina, "Psychological Correlates of the Reading Process." Presented at International Reading Association Conference, May, 1962.
23. Dozier, Paul, "The Neurological Background of Word Deafness." *The Bulletin of the Orton Society*, Vol. III, 1958.
24. Drake, Charles, "Time for a New Look at the 'Minimal Brain Damage' Hypothesis." *International Approach to Learning Disabilities of Children and Youth*, The Association for Children With Learning Disabilities, Inc., 1966.
25. Dunsing, Jack and Newell Kephart, "Motor Generalizations in Space and Time." LEARNING DISORDERS, Vol. I., edited by J. Hellmuth. Special Child Publications, Seattle, 1965.
26. Eisenberg, Leon, "The Epidemiology of Reading Retardation and a Program for Preventive Intervention." THE DISABLED READER, edited by John Money. Baltimore, The Johns Hopkins Press, 1966.
27. Ellingson, Careth, THE SHADOW CHILDREN: *A Book About Children's Learning Disorders*. Chicago, Topaz Books, 1967.
28. Flower, Richard M., Helen Gofman, Lucie Lawson, READING DISORDERS, *A Multi-Sensory Symposium*. Philadelphia, F.A. Davis, 1965.
29. Frostig, Marianne, and David Horne, "An Approach to the Treatment of Children with Learning Disorders." LEARNING DISORDERS, Vol. I, edited by J. Hellmuth. Special Child Publications, Seattle, 1965.
30. Gallagher, J. Roswell, "Can't Spell, Can't Read." *The Atlantic Monthly,* 1948 (an Orton Society reprint).
31. ———"Specific Language Disability: Dyslexia." *The Bulletin of the Orton Society*, Vol. XIII, 1963 (an Orton Society reprint).
32. Gillingham, Anna, and Bessie Stillman, REMEDIAL TRAINING FOR CHILDREN WITH SPECIFIC DISABILITY IN READING, SPELLING, AND PENMANSHIP. Cambridge, Mass., Educators Publishing Service, Inc., 1956, 1960.
33. Gillingham, Anna, "The Obligation of the School to Teach Reading and Spelling—A Challenge." *The Independent School Bulletin,* April, 1955.
34. ———"Is Writing Essential for Proof of Knowledge?" *The Independent School Bulletin*, November, 1958.
35. ——— EDUCATION AND SPECIFIC LANGUAGE DISABILITY: *The papers of Anna Gillingham*, compiled by Sally B. Childs. The Orton Society, Monograph 3, 1968.
36. Goldberg, Herman Krieger, "Neurological Aspects of Reading Problems." Pennsylvania Academy of Ophthalmology and Otolaryngology, Transactions, Spring, 1965.
37. Hellmuth, Jerome, editor, LEARNING DISORDERS, Vol. I. Seattle, Special Child Publications, 1965.
38. ——— LEARNING DISORDERS, Vol. II. Seattle, Special Child Publications, 1966.

39. _____ EDUCATIONAL THERAPY, Vol. I. Seattle, Special Child Publications, 1966.

40. Hermann, Knud, READING DISABILITY. Springfield, Ill., Charles C. Thomas, 1959.

41. Johnson, Doris, and Helmer R. Myklebust, LEARNING DISABILITIES. New York and London, Grune and Stratton, Inc., 1967.

42. _____"Dyslexia in Childhood." LEARNING DISORDERS, Vol. I, edited by J. Hellmuth. Seattle, Special Child Publications, 1965.

43. Keeney, Arthur H. and Virginia T. Keeney, *Dyslexia: Diagnosis and Treatment of Reading Disorders*. St. Louis, C.V. Nosby, 1968.

44. Kephart, Newell, THE SLOW LEARNER IN THE CLASSROOM. Columbus, Ohio, Charles E. Merrill Books, 1960.

45. _____"Perceptual-Motor Aspects of Learning Disabilities." *Exceptional Children*, December, 1964.

46. Kline, Carl, READING DISABILITIES—*Historical Perspectives, Diagnosis and Therapy*. A 900 foot tape, P.O. Box 6385, Postal Station G, Vancouver 8, B.C., Canada.

47. Koppitz, Elizabeth M., THE BENDER GESTALT TEST FOR YOUNG CHILDREN. New York and London, Grune and Stratton, Inc., 1964.

48. Krech, David, "The Chemistry of Learning." *Saturday Review*, January 20, 1968.

49. Martin, Bill Jr., SOUNDS OF LANGUAGE SERIES. New York, Holt, Rinehart & Winston, Inc.

50. Masland, Richard L., "Brain Mechanism Underlying the Language Function." *The Bulletin of The Orton Society*, Vol. XVII, 1967 (an Orton Society reprint).

51. Money, John, editor, READING DISABILITY: PROGRESS AND RESEARCH IN DYSLEXIA. Baltimore, The Johns Hopkins Press, 1962.

52. Money, John, and Gilbert Schiffman, THE DISABLED READER. Baltimore, The Johns Hopkins Press, 1966.

53. Myklebust, Helmer R., AUDITORY DISORDERS IN CHILDREN. New York and London, Grune and Stratton, Inc., 1954.

54. Norrie, Edith, "Word Blindness in Denmark: Its Neurological and Educational Aspects." *The Independent School Bulletin,* April, 1960.

55. Orton, June L., A GUIDE TO TEACHING PHONICS. Cambridge, Mass., Educators Publishing Service, Inc., 1964, 1973.

56. _____"The Orton-Gillingham Approach." THE DISABLED READER, edited by J. Money and G. Schiffman. Baltimore, The Johns Hopkins Press, 1966.

57. Orton, Samuel T., READING, WRITING AND SPEECH PROBLEMS IN CHILDREN. New York, W.W. Norton and Company, 1937.

58. _____ WORD BLINDNESS IN SCHOOL CHILDREN. And other papers compiled by June Lyday Orton, The Orton Society, Monograph 2, 1966.

59. Penfield, Wilder, and Lamar Roberts, SPEECH AND BRAIN-MECHANISM. Princeton, Princeton University Press, 1959.

60. _____"The Uncommitted Cortex." *The Atlantic Monthly*, July, 1964.

61. Piaget, Jean, THE ORIGINS OF INTELLIGENCE IN CHILDREN. New York, International Universities Press, 1952.

62. Rabinovitch, Ralph D., "Dyslexia: Psychiatric Considerations." READING DISABILITY, edited by J. Money. Baltimore, The Johns Hopkins Press, 1962.

63. _____"Neuropsychiatric Considerations in Reading Retardation." *The Reading Teacher*, May, 1962.

64. Rawson, Margaret, DEVELOPMENTAL LANGUAGE DISABILITY—*Adult Accomplishments of Dyslexic Boys*. Baltimore, The Johns Hopkins Press, 1968.

65. _____ A BIBLIOGRAPHY OF THE NATURE, RECOGNITION AND TREATMENT OF LANGUAGE DIFFICULTIES. Cambridge, Mass., Educators Publishing Service, Inc., 1966, 1969, 1974.

66. Richards, Mary Helen, THRESHOLD TO MUSIC. New York, Harper and Row.

67. Rosner, Stanley, "Ophthalmology, Optometry, and Learning Difficulties." *Journal of Learning Disabilities*, Vol. I, No. 8, August, 1968.

68. Rucker, W. Ray, Clyde Arnspiger and Arthur J. Brodbeck, HUMAN VALUES IN EDUCATION. Dubuque, Iowa, Wm. C. Brown Book Co., 1969.

69. _____ THE HUMAN VALUE SERIES. Steck-Vaughn Co., P.O. Box 2028, Austin, Texas.

70. Saunders, Roger E., "Dyslexia: Its Phenomenology." READING DISABILITY, edited by John Money. Baltimore, The Johns Hopkins Press, 1962 (an Orton Society reprint).

71. Schiffman, Gilbert, "Dyslexia as an Educational Phenomenon: Its Recognition and Treatment." READING DISABILITY, edited by John Money. Baltimore, The Johns Hopkins Press, 1962.

72. _____"Early Identification of Reading Disabilities." *Bulletin of the Orton Society*, Vol. XIV, 1964.

73. Silver, Archie A., and Rosa A. Hagin, "Specific Reading Disability: An Approach to Diagnosis and Treatment". *The Journal of Special Education*, Vol. I, No. 2.

74. _____"Specific Reading Disability: Follow-up Studies." *American Journal of Orthopsychiatry*, January 1, 1964.

75. Silver, Archie A., "Strategies of Intervention in the Spectrum of Defects in Specific Reading Disability." *The Bulletin of the Orton Society,* Vol. XVII, 1967 (an Orton Society reprint).

76. _____"Diagnostic Considerations in Children with Reading Disability." *The Bulletin of the Orton Society*, Vol. XI, 1961 (an Orton Society reprint).

77. Slingerland, Beth H., TRAINING IN SOME PREREQUISITES FOR BEGINNING READING. Cambridge, Mass., Educators Publishing Service, Inc., 1967.

78. _____"Public School Programs for the Prevention of Specific Language Disability in Children." EDUCATIONAL THERAPY, Vol. I, edited by J. Hellmuth. Seattle, Special Child Publications, 1966.

79. _____ SCREENING TESTS FOR IDENTIFYING CHILDREN WITH SPECIFIC LANGUAGE DISABILITIES. Cambridge, Mass., Educators Publishing Service, Inc., 1964, 1970, 1974.

80. _____ PRE-READING SCREENING PROCEDURES. Cambridge, Mass., Educators Publishing Service, Inc., 1969.

81. _____"A Public School Program of Prevention for Young Children With Specific Language Disability." The Orton Society, Monograph 1, 1964.

82. _____"Meeting the Needs of Dyslexic Children." *Academic Therapy Quarterly*, Vol. I, No. 2, 1966.

83. _____ "Early Identification of Pre-School Children Who Might Fail." *Academic Therapy Quarterly*, Summer, 1969.

84. Stuart, Marion F., NEUROPHYSIOLOGICAL INSIGHTS INTO TEACHING. Palo Alto, Calif., Pacific Books, 1963.

85. _____ "Specific Language Disabilities—What Are They?" *Academic Therapy Quarterly*, Vol. I, No. 3.

86. Subirana, Antonio, "The Problem of Cerebral Dominance: The Relationship Between Handedness and Language Function." *Logos*, 4:12, October, 1961, and reprinted in *The Bulletin of the Orton Society*, Vol. XIV, 1964.

87. Tompkins, Calvin, "The Last Skill Acquired." By the "Reporter at Large" in *The New Yorker,* September 14, 1963.

88. Thompson, Lloyd J., READING DISABILITY—*Developmental Dyslexia*. Springfield, Ill., Charles C. Thomas, 1966.

89. Thompson, Lloyd J., "Concepts of Learning Disabilities." *North Carolina Medical Journal*, Vol. 29, No. 11, Nov. 1968.

90. Waites, Lucius and Aylett Cox, DEVELOPMENTAL LANGUAGE DISABILITY —BASIC TRAINING—REMEDIAL LANGUAGE TRAINING. Cambridge, Mass., Educators Publishing Service, Inc., 1969.

91. Wepman, Joseph M., "Dyslexia: Its Relationship to Language Acquisition and Concept Formation." READING DISABILITY, edited by John Money. Baltimore, The Johns Hopkins Press, 1962.

92. Whitsell, Leon J., "Delacato's 'Neurological Organization': A Medical Appraisal." *California School Health*, Vol. 3, No. 3, Fall, 1967.

93. _____ "Neurological Aspects of Reading Disorders." READING DISORDERS, edited by Flower, Gofman, Lawson. Philadelphia, F. A. Davis Company, 1965.

BULLETINS

*The Bulletin of the Orton Society,* The Orton Society, Inc.
8415 Bellona Lane
Towson, Maryland 21204
(reprints available)

*Word Blind Bulletin* Word Blind Clinic
The General Secretary, Invalid Children's Aid Association
126 Buckingham Palace Road
London, S.W. 1, England

*Journal of Learning Disabilities*
5 North Wabash Ave.
Chicago, Ill. 60602

*Academic Therapy - a Quarterly*
San Rafael, California 94901